HERITAGE '

CW01661760

A collection of st

about

people, places and events

of

yesterday and today

in

Cullen Deskford and Portknockie

This book is a sample of the research and writings of members of the group since it was formed in 1990.

Published by Cullen Deskford and Portknockie Heritage Group
Printed by MMS Almac Ltd, Keith

ISBN 0 9530545 0 0

FOREWORD

by

The Rt. Hon. The Earl of Seafield

I was most greatly honoured to have been asked by the Cullen, Deskford and Portknockie Heritage Group to write a short foreword to this book

It is vitally important for any community to have records for posterity which are available for future generations to read, so that they understand and know what took place in the past and how, in some cases, it effected the present. We should all be grateful to the individuals of The Cullen, Deskford and Portknockie Heritage Group who have shown the initiative, and taken the trouble to see that future generations will have the knowledge of what went on in this area in the past and present.

History is more than just a series of social and political upheavals, interspersed with battles and invasions. There is no way for future generations to understand the social fabric of the areas in which they live unless they have some idea of what happened in the past. Very often too little attention has been paid to this aspect of History and in this instance this fault is being rectified by selfless individuals who show that they really care about the local community in which they live.

I urge you to read on therefore, you will not be bored!

CONTENTS

Acknowledgements

The Cullen Deskford and Portknockie Heritage Group would like to express their thanks to the many people who have guided, helped and encouraged them with the production of this book.

The Management Committee of Cullen Community Education Centre initiated the Group in 1990 and they deserve a special mention. They showed their confidence, gave their encouragement and very importantly gave their financial backing at a very early stage to the idea of producing a book.

The Moray District Library Service has been of great help to the Group since its early days by providing, through its libraries, an outlet for the writings of the members to the general public.

The Group appreciates very much the financial support given by way of grants by several organisations and acknowledge that without this support this book could not have been produced. Those who gave grants were Grampian Enterprise Limited through their Leader II Scheme, Rural Initiative (Scotland), Royal Burgh of Cullen and Deskford Community Council and Cullen Common Good Fund through the Moray Council.

The Earl of Seafield has kindly written the Foreword to this book and the Group are grateful for his interest and support.

There are many from outside the Group who have been of great help and who have given of their valuable time willingly. One person in particular has been such a pillar of support that he cannot escape being named - Alastair Wilson who was invited to join the Book Committee to give the "outsider" opinion. He gave much good advice and also played a valuable part in proof-reading. The Manager of the Libraries and Museums of Moray Council, Alistair Campbell has encouraged the Group and has been unfailing in his support.

Many of the photographs used in the book were donated to the Group and every effort has been made to obtain the permission of the donors to use them. Thanks are due to those who have made photographs available for inclusion in the book.

Lastly but most importantly are the members of the Group who have researched their subjects and produced what we hope readers will find interesting stories. If these stories stir memories and bring a quiet smile to the face, a little bit tear to the eye or a lump in the throat, particularly if the reader is far from home, then the efforts of everyone who contributed to the writing of this book will have been well worth while.

Heritage in Cullen Deskford and Portknockie

Back in 1990 the Management Committee of the Cullen Community Education Centre decided to sponsor a group to record the heritage of Cullen and the surrounding area. From a small number of enthusiasts, the group has grown to around thirty members who meet monthly to discuss amongst themselves the research work they have done. Sometimes this is in the form of a formal presentation of something a member has researched. If it is a written item, it may be read by the author or by someone else. The subject may be of the author's choice or selected from a list of subjects which the group thinks are worth researching. Alternatively it could be an audio tape recording of the memories of an elderly person or a video of some of the features of the surrounding countryside. Guest speakers come along from time to time to add variety and whether the presenter is one of the group or from outwith, lively discussion and sometimes argument ensues!

The group also gathers "memorabilia" such as newspaper cuttings of past events, programmes, pamphlets and things like wartime ration books. These are carefully stored after being recorded and cross-referenced for easy finding. This is an area of work which is very time-consuming, particularly to keep it up to date.

The group has also amassed a large collection of photographs, mainly donated by members of the public who are anxious to ensure that photographs which have perhaps been in their possession for many years will be preserved for posterity. The group operates a "borrow, copy and return" scheme so that people can keep their photographs but make them available for a wider viewing. This scheme is expensive to operate but very necessary.

The written work is recorded in the group's own computer and copies made available to the public in folders kept by the local libraries. These are kept up to date and are well used by local people, students and visitors. Access to archive material can be arranged through the library.

The group has no facilities for the storage of big items of heritage, such as butter churns and other household items from yesterday. Maybe some day.....!

It is a saying amongst those involved in heritage that today's events are tomorrow's heritage. But tomorrow's heritage can easily be lost when memories fade and people die, if today's events are not recorded either on paper, on tape or film negatives. So often people think "Nothing has ever happened to me worth speaking about" but it is not true - everyone has a tale to tell !

Members of the Cullen Deskford and Portknockie Heritage Group will be glad to hear of anyone who has a tale to tell or has special knowledge of some past event.

TWICE DAILY ROUND THE BOTHY

(AN INCOMER'S VIEW OF CULLEN)

by Gladys Leith

Gladys Leith hails from Northumberland and is a founder member of the Heritage Group. She is the Scribe of the group, putting material written by members on to the computer and is very interested in the local language and customs. She has clearly taken Cullen to her heart.

In 1985 when I first came to live here, with my beautiful black labrador dog Calum I began to explore the areas around Cullen. We used to walk down to the Seatown, along the beach, over the rocks and up the path to the cliff top at Portknockie, then back along the cliffs, down a path, across the golf course, along the sea front, up a path above the harbour and home.

In time, after a few discreet questions, the locals had discovered "fa' I wis an' far I bade" and I realised that Calum and I were becoming "weel kent" figures. The greetings became more friendly - we were greeted with "Aye aye, fit like?" and when I said that I was well and enquired how they were, the reply was either "Fine" or "Nae bad", so I supposed that if you were neither of these - and I've never met anyone who was worse than nae bad - you were not fit to be out of doors and must at least be confined to the house!

Calum

We were becoming more familiar with the area and now we walked across the Cullen Burn, paused at the Staples, the rocks at the foot of the burn to watch a stately heron fishing or sea birds preening. Then we continued along the beach, past the Three Kings rocks, the Boar Craig and Black Foot, the Den Burn - sometimes a trickle, sometimes quite a flood - and lastly over the Cruats Burn. Then between the rocks where if the tide is high it can become necessary to scramble round the higher rocks or get wet feet. Calum found it was nae bother at all! Past Preacher's Cave to Jenny's Well where in summer time the air is filled with the scent of balsam. I have been told that Jenny's Well is named after a tinker woman Janet Carstairs who about 1840 lived in a nearby cave. I had hoped that the painstakingly marked out name meant the declaration of someone's undying love!

Often a seal can be spotted perched on a rounded rock. One day, near Jenny's Well, a retired skipper from Portknockie pointed out to me seven large stones, which he said marked a human grave. I often stand at the stones and wonder!

A pech (sorry - a breathless climb) up the path past the Whale's Moo', and then a rest on the seat to look back and enjoy the lovely view of Cullen Bay, the Bin and the surrounding countryside and the rocky coast line. Then back along the cliff tops, down the Reed Roadie, across the golf course, retracing our steps along the beach, along the Back o' the Toon, past the Harbour, up Pitness Brae and home - or should it be hame!

Soon the Salmon Bothy walk became an established favourite, no need to worry about high tides here. Where once I saw primroses and seagulls, I now see spinkies and pewles, the local name so describes their call. Sometimes we would go to Nelson's Point, hoping the louper dogs would swim by - entertaining us as only dolphins can.

We were totally exposed to the elements, often the wind had a cutting edge to it with horizontal hailstones lashing us, often rainbows shining above us and often the sea like a mill-pond.

But no matter what the weather had to offer, Calum and I went "oot aboot". We watched the fishing boats leaving or returning with their catch, the local lobster boatmen attending to their creels, sailing boats, huge oil tankers and oil rigs tended occasionally by sea-going tugs.

There was always plenty to see. We watched dolphins and seals, listened to the gentle cooing of the male eider ducks at courtship and later watched their young, escorted by the females, managing to remain on the surface of the sea, which to human eyes, is seemingly too rough for their tiny bodies. We saw shore birds and sea birds in all the seasons, but one of the most exciting things is to hear the wild geese flying overhead and to watch them as in their hundreds they fly north to begin their breeding season - spring is on the wing! Then to see the eagerly awaited arrival of the swallow and to hear the wonderful song of the skylark. We saw many beautiful plants and flowers and bats at dusk.

Near some fresh water at the Bothy in the summer, the lovely smell of Meadow Sweet fills the air - and can it still be the same jenny wren that resided in the blackthorn last year?

My lovely Calum is no longer with me and now my walks are less frequent but I like to think that perhaps a silent and unseen companion is with me when I take my walks - either in reality or just in my mind's eye - "Twice daily round the Bothy".

VOICES FROM THE PAST

by Douglas Summers

Douglas Summers is a founder member of the Heritage Group, a retired Art teacher. His speciality in the Heritage Group is sound recording and in this short article he tells of some of his more interesting recordings and of the people who made them.

Amongst the many recordings I have made of the voices of interesting people, one that has given me particular pleasure is that of Mrs Clara Inglis, a wonderful lady who was almost 80 when she recorded stories of her young days. She lived in a bygone age and was in service in the days when the big houses, such as Cullen House, had many servants who lived and worked in a very structured way. Clara Inglis had a wonderful memory and was a very fluent speaker, well able to hold the attention of any listener. One day in 1983 I went to her Lintmill home taking with me a recorder and a 90 minute cassette tape, but she told stories, without stopping, for all of two and a half hours! I lost a great many fascinating anecdotes and foolishly, I failed to go back for further recording before she died in 1994. I can give only a brief indication of some of Clara's stories here - they are really best listened to.

Clara Inglis

When she was a very young girl, about six years old, Clara Inglis knew some of the staff of Cullen House where she used to visit the kitchen. Sometimes she helped by making the morning toast for the Countess. One day the Countess asked "Who is making my toast?". When she was told it was Farquhar's daughter, she asked to see Clara who was "....just enchanted. I didna' half get a scrub, I'm telling you but I was dressed an' I was that feart I wid file ma sheen that I carried them". The housekeeper took Clara in and the Countess asked if she made the toast. She answered "Yes, my lady. And if there is one broken, I'll ait it masel!". She told the Countess that she would like to be a cook and was thrilled at being given a pound note, some other gifts including a stuffed parrot, and also an invitation to come back sometime. Sadly the Countess died shortly afterwards, in 1911. Later, as an employee, Clara used to put on the fire in the room underneath the Temple when the "toffs" went bathing. She tells another story about going with a friend to see a travelling menagerie in Cullen Square, recalling the fun they had there and of seeing "...wild beasts o' a' kines!".

Another memorable recording is that of Mrs Edith Beveridge, widow of Mr J A Beveridge, headmaster of Deskford School, around the time of and after the Second World War. Edith Beveridge was well acquainted with Deskford, having been born, brought up and lived most of her life in the parish. Her memories went back to the early 1900's and she had stories about the Church, the Sunday School, her schooldays in Deskford and Buckie, the farms and the way of life in her early years.

There is also a recording of Sam Munro telling of how tiles, drainpipes and flower pots were made in the tile works at Lintmill. He recalled how, as a boy, he used to walk through the works on his way to collect milk for his family and he described how the furnaces glowed as the bricks were being fired.

Sadly, of the three above people none is still living. It is, however, of great historical value that we have these stories, personal memories, told in their own words, with the distinctiveness of their own voices, by those who experienced a different way of life now gone. It is important that we preserve records of former everyday activities and customs of our community before those memories and voices are lost forever. Among other items we have, for instance, a description by Dr Ian Ralston, formerly of Aberdeen University, of an archaeological dig, worked over several years during the 1980's, on top of the Green Castle, Portknockie. He tells of finding evidence of the site having been used for various purposes from the late 1800's back for 2500 years.

Many people enjoy hearing these voices from the past. I enjoy and am grateful for the privilege of meeting people and recording their voices for posterity.

Copies of the recordings are in the Heritage Group records and are used on occasions when the work of the group is on public display, for instance when the group attends Rurals and Guilds etc. or arranges outside demonstrations.

HOW MARY BETTERED THE FACTOR

Mary was tenant of a small croft. She was what was called an 'ootman'. She kept cattle and barrowed her own turnips from the field. She did get Dad to do the ploughing and that kind of thing, but she was very independent. Mary wanted a bit of ground to garden, to grow her tatties in. The Factor came up and some of the other Cullen House people - it was quite an occasion. Dad was there of course and much to his amusement at one point Mary said she wanted a fence round her garden. "Oh but" the Factor said "the estate's had so many expenses..." and he elaborated on that. Mary listened quite patiently, then she said "'Deed Sir, it's maybe a' true 'at ye say, but there's little o't come my wye!". Mary got her fence!

TOCHIENEAL DISTILLERY

by John Rennie

John Rennie, a retired electrician lives in Portknockie and has a great interest in the heritage of the area. As well as being a member of the Cullen Deskford and Portknockie Heritage Group he is a member of the Buckie Fishing Heritage which has its headquarters at the rear of the Buckie Library. He specialises in video recording and has done much to put material on computer and to organise the group's photographic collection.

Between the years 1820 and 1824 Tochieneal Distillery was built by Alexander Wilson who for nearly thirty years was Factor for Seafield Estates, Cullen. The Wilsons, originally from Brangan near Portsoy were a prominent farming family who leased several farms in the district, were members of Cullen Town Council, and provided three Factors for Seafield Estates.

The distillery flourished and in 1828 an expansion of the premises was completed. The average annual quantity of spirits distilled from malt were 25,292 gallons at proof. Annual average duty paid on spirits and malt £5188.

When Alexander Wilson died in 1831 his nephews, Alexander (Sandy) and John, who was also a Factor for Seafield Estates and founder of the Tochieneal Tile Works took over the various leases including the distillery which was managed by Sandy. Sandy also held the lease of Kilnhillock farm till 1876, although he lived most of the time at Tochieneal.

John Wilson died in 1852 aged fifty. Sandy then continued to run the farms, tile works and distillery, while also acting as Factor under Seafield Estates cashier, W. G. Bryson. Unfortunately there was a clash of personalities between Sandy and John Charles who succeeded as 7th Earl in 1853 and this led to Sandy's resignation in 1854. This appears to have been the beginning of a rift between the Wilson family and Seafield Estates.

Part of the old buildings at Tochieneal which were quite extensive (see plan) still remain and are situated between the village of Lintmill and the steading at Tochieneal farm. They are well preserved and probably had been the grain lofts and barns. There are the remains of some gearing and a filled-in lade on the road side of the building along with several stones protruding from the wall which supported the water chutes feeding the water wheel. Apparently the cast iron water wheel was broken up and used for the war effort. In 1870 the year before the lease of the distillery was due to expire the Countess of Seafield raised objections to the presence

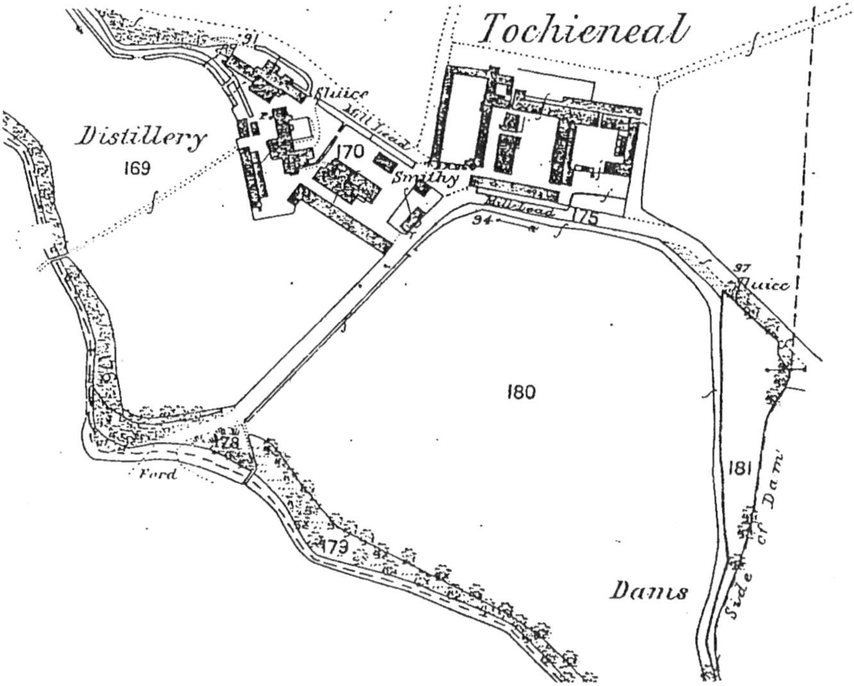

Plan of Tochineal Distillery

of the distillery on her lands and doubled the rent. Because of this problem, along with the need for further expansion and possibly because of problems with a pure and plentiful water supply, Sandy Wilson decided to give up the lease and find another site for the distillery. He eventually found the ideal site with a pure and plentiful water supply at Inchgower near Buckie. Sandy then left Tochieneal, and for a time lived at Kilnhillock farmhouse, east of Cullen with his sister Jessie. When the distillery was built in 1871 he moved to Arradoul House near Inchgower.

The poem reproduced here mentions some of the workers names and their thoughts on moving from Tochieneal to Inchgower.

TOCHIENEAL

Come a' my young lads, ye'll mak haste and be ready
for May twenty-sax will be here in a crack
An' we ane and a' but the man in the smiddy
maun leave Tochieneal, nae mair tae come back.

Awa to the west we maun a' gang th'gither
the men, wives and wee anes, wi' true herts and leal
An our wives they will a' be in a sad swither
on that awfu day, that we leave Tochieneal.

Aucht wives in a hoose wi a brick separation
I niver ance thocht it wad dee verra weel
for their tongues were sair neid for tae gie provocation
there cou'd be nae contentment at auld Tochieneal.

There were Jamie and Sandy, and Archie and Wattie
there were Walker and Taylor, and Forbes and Kemp
we were aucht jolly lads, but we're jist something chatty
when ance we get in the wee drappie o' drink.

We're aul, and we're wracket, to work w'ed nae scruple
our joints they are stiff and that we do feel
they're no like our wives tongues, for faith they're richt supple
when they think we've been drinking the pure Tochieneal.

But what is a' this but a blether o' nonsense
there's nane o's been there yet that grievance to feel
but there's ae thing I'll say, without hurting my conscience
the bye-word will be - this is nae Tochineal.

When the distillery closed, most of the plant stock and machinery was shifted to Inchgower including the clock which is still in use at the distillery. There also still exists in the reception area a copper flagon with a brass plate marked "Tochieneal". Sandy Wilson was joined by nephews, John and James Wilson at Inchgower. Sandy Wilson died in 1882 and Walter Wilson, along with two other members of the Wilson family were the last private owners. Provost Merson led the Buckie Town Council when Inchgower distillery was bought in 1929 for £1000. It sold in 1936 for £6000, a not insignificant profit!

SOME INTERESTING NOTES

John Forbes, Maryhill Farm, Hill of Maud, Deskford, a descendant of Forbes mentioned in the poem owns a small barrel - capacity about one gallon - made by

Forbes who was a cooper at the distillery at Tochieneal. Apparently it was the custom then to have the barrel filled with whisky each New Year.

The clock from Tochieneal Distillery was made by William Mortimer clock maker in Cullen or it may have been made by his nephew William who worked with his uncle and later set up business in Portsoy.

Mr M. J. Walker, Headmaster of Cullen School is a direct descendant of the Walker mentioned in the poem Tochieneal. His father, born 1911 was a son of Alexander Walker who married Helen Stuart. Her father was brewer at Inchgower. Alexander, whose father had worked at Tochieneal returned there after his first son was born at Inchgower around 1878 and was employed as gardener at Tochieneal House. It is believed that his wife Helen used to walk to Inchgower from Tochieneal with the children to visit her father, returning on the stagecoach to Cullen if money was available for the fare. Alexander later became gardener at the Linn Home in Keith where he laid out the garden in a style similar to the one at Tochieneal.

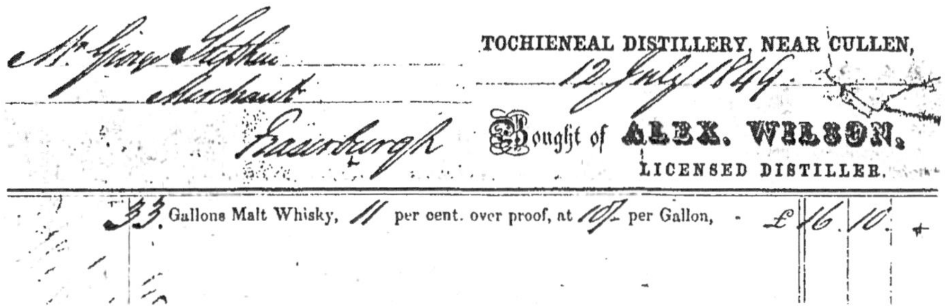
Mr George Stephen
Merchant
Fraserburgh
TOCHIENEAL DISTILLERY, NEAR CULLEN,
12 July 1844
Bought of ALEX. WILSON,
LICENSED DISTILLER.
33 Gallons Malt Whisky, 11 per cent. over proof, at 10/- per Gallon, - £16.10.

Invoice from Tochieneal Distillery

Dr JAMES CAMPBELL LL.D.

Dr Campbell was Factor of Seafield Estates and took a very active part in local affairs. He served on Burgh and Parish Councils, he was Deputy Lieutenant and Convenor of the County of Banff, and represented Cullen at the General Assembly of the Church of Scotland in Edinburgh.

He is well remembered as a benefactor and donated a house for convalescent soldiers, still known as Campbell House, although now used as flats. He made a substantial contribution to the cost of building Campbell Hospital in Portsoy. In recognition of his many public services he was granted the Freedom of the Burgh in 1912 and knighted.

CLAY AND DASH HOUSES IN PORTKNOCKIE

by William Slater

William Slater is a Portknockie man who, apart from war service in the Royal Air Force has spent most of his life in his home town. After some time working as a joiner he ran a carpet and hardware business until his retirement.

My first memory of an old thatched house in Portknockie was when my mother sent me to collect vegetables from an old man called "Knoxie" who, I suppose sold vegetables for a living. I was amazed as I had never seen a house like it before.

It was a very old clay and dash house with a thatched roof, two tiny windows and a door in two halves, horizontally. Inside was just as basic. There was a bare earthen floor sprinkled with sand. There was a chimney but no fireplace or grate of any kind. For furniture they had a chest of drawers, a cupboard for a primitive wardrobe, the bed was a bag of chaff on a wooden frame, a few kitchen utensils and that was it! The last thatched house of this kind was on Mid Street and was demolished around 1928.

In my quest for information about houses built with round stones, clay and straw, I have found that there are no written records. What I know comes from word-of-mouth stories. The first thing that puzzled me was why did they use round stones (difficult to build with) using clay and straw, when stone and lime houses were already going up in Cullen? The answer was of course cost! The moors around Portknockie were being cleared of stones to form pasture land and these stones were free. The clay was readily available from several nearby "clay pots" and there was a surplus of straw so everything was free and to hand!

No foundations were made as in later buildings. The walls were built directly on the earth and were made by laying the larger stones a wall-width apart with timber on the outside as shuttering and the space between filled with the stone, clay and straw mixture. The wet clay and straw slurry was poured in first, then the stones added, making sure they were well coated so that there were no air pockets. This mixture did not have to cure like concrete as there was no chemical reaction - as soon as it was dry it was ready.

In the construction of clay and dash houses with thatched roofs, the first lift was up to the windowsills and this was left to dry before the second lift, up to the eaves at about 6 feet high was laid. A long piece of timber was laid across the wall to form lintels for the windows and doors. Finally the walls were coated with lime to

Typical Clay and Dash Cottage in Portknockie

make them waterproof. Besides waterproofing, the lime coating gave the house an improved appearance as the accompanying photograph shows.

The roof was next. The probable method of roof building then was similar to what I saw on the very old buildings I had to strip as an apprentice joiner. The rafters were young trees simply halved down the middle and fixed with two cut nails at top and bottom. This method would be dated about 1850. The rafters were secured lengthways by lighter sticks and the thatch of straw laid on these and tied down. It was essential that the wall-heads were well covered to prevent penetration of water on to the clay. Often ropes were laid over the roof and held down by heavy stones to stop the entire roof lifting in the wind. Once the roof was on, the interior earth was dug out to a depth of 6 to 8 inches and the earth replaced with sand for the floor.

A partition was put across the interior to divide it in two. Into this was put a built-in bed (bunnen bed), usually quite small, about 5 feet 8 inches long by 4 feet wide and this, unlike the rest of the interior had a roof. This roof was used as a store for clothes, often under a piece of old sail. Cooking utensils were kept under the bed along with such items as boots. This part of the house was called the "ben", and the family lived there most of the time. If the family was comparatively well-off there would be wall-to-wall flagstones, and sometimes a wooden floor with logs cut lengthwise laid in the sand and planked. The open fire had a "lum" which was a wooden-sided aperture in the roof to let the smoke out. A later improvement was a chimney which carried the smoke from the fire to the "lum". The other part of the house was the "but" and it had to have a sand floor because, if the weather was too wet to bait the fishing lines outside, it was done in the "but" under cover. This entailed opening mussels which contained a lot of water which seeped into the sand. This eventually created some smell and the sand was changed, now and then.

Later, larger houses were made with both quarried and round stones, again using the clay and straw mixture. As before there were no foundations but a base of large stones was set out and the smaller ones built in layers or courses. Only two courses were laid in one day as more weight would squeeze out the clay mixture. The walls again had to be sheltered from rain until dry and then coated with lime. There are still many houses of this sort where extra height has been added with stone and lime mortar.

When larger fishing boats came, stones were needed for ballast. These were emptied out when fishing and then replaced with quarried stones, often ones which were blocked at the quarry at Pulteney (part of Wick). Pulteney Street in Portknockie was named after this quarry. Once the railway came to Portknockie, stone was readily available from many different places, even from granite quarries. The last houses I remember being built from Portknockie stone were the council houses in Samson Street. George Paul the mason once told me he went to Durn Quarry himself to get the stones for Mariner House in Portknockie.

TONY HETHERINGTON

Tony Hetherington was born in Reading and came to Cullen in 1978 and soon became a very popular figure in the town. He started to train as an engineer but switched to Philosophy and graduated from Aberdeen University. In 1993 he was working on a project at Ladysbridge Hospital near Banff before he left on a canoeing holiday in Austria with club members from Moray. While attempting to negotiate a stretch of rapids, his canoe overturned and he was drowned. He was unmarried and aged 44.

He will be remembered for his single-handed reconstruction of his small house in Seatown, turning a ruin into a charming home. But his greatest achievement was his work in improving the "Giant Steps" on the coastal path east of Cullen, a task involving the placing of huge stones entirely by muscle power. While engaged on this Herculean task he imposed on himself a vow of silence and his achievement was marked after his death by a plaque on a stone cairn erected by the people of Cullen.

CULLEN IN ITS "HOLIDAY RESORT" DAYS

by Sandra Taylor

Sandra Taylor is a Cullen lass who has spent much of her adult life in the Central Belt of Scotland. She is Minute Secretary of the Group and an active contributor to the Group's work. Here she recalls her early days in Cullen when the "visitors" played an important part in the economy of the town.

Cullen today still attracts holiday-makers, but its heyday was without doubt in the 30s, 40s. and 50s, before the age of the motor car and package holidays. "Visitors" arrived by the train load and Clarkie Merson, driver of the railway lorry had full-time employment delivering their cases and hampers to the hotels, guest houses and private dwelling houses which then became their holiday homes. Home-owners let their property with or without attendance. The latter often involved moving the family into "the shed", usually a sizeable outhouse adapted for temporary living. Others took in sleepers - a mutually suitable arrangement with a hotel or guest house to provide sleeping facilities only where there was an overspill, the hotel or guest house providing the meals. The Links and beach thronged with people. Bathing, for safety reasons was restricted to an area between two strings of corks. Changing took place in a row of purpose-built huts, the most westerly one of which was used to store a large number of deck chairs which were hired out. In charge of the hiring in the earlier days was Jeannie Innes, assisted by Jessie Ross, and later on Barbara Jessie took over with her big black leather bag. Glasgow Fair, the busiest period, was synoymous with the Christian Endeavourers, who brought their Seaside Mission to Cullen from 1948 till 1969. "Grandpa Jenkins" and his team are still spoken of with affection, such was the huge impression they made, through their activities, on the lives of countless youngsters. Uncle Andy, Uncle Duff, Uncle Richard and Uncle Jack conjure up memories of seaside services, sand-building competitions and fancy dress parades. Hymn singing took place each night at the harbour and drew large crowds. On a beautiful summer evening at sunset, it was a poignant experience, one never forgotten by those who attended. Many "visitors" returned to Cullen year after year, and friendships - very often lifelong - were forged on the sands, at the harbour, on the bowling green or golf course - or simply "claikin'" at the Back o' the Toon.

Jessie and Jeannie

SPORTS AND AMUSEMENTS OF THE PAST

by Isobel Gray

Isobel Gray is a retired secondary school teacher who has lived nearly all her life in Cullen. Her father was Provost of Cullen for fifteen years and she is much involved with the church and the Guide movement. After being appointed Commissioner, a post she held for many years she is now President of Moray Guides.

Today practically every home has a television set and on average, people watch T. V. sixteen hours per week, so out of a life span of three score years and ten, they spend six years watching a screen rather than doing anything. So how did people use their spare time in those far-off days before television and videos took such a hold on their lives?

Let me begin with children. The young ones played indoor games in their own homes with their brothers, sisters and parents - Ludo, Happy Families, snakes and ladders, dominoes, draughts, and so on. As they grew older they tended to make and operate things; the boys Meccano, fretwork and chemistry sets and the girls sewing, scrap books and such-like.

The younger generation learn to skip as their parents did in days of yore

Out of doors they had lots of activities and most of the time they created their own amusement and they did things. Depending on the season of the year, they played different games - some individual and some organised. There was a time for skipping, groups at break times played skipping games in the playground, two turning a heavy rope while the rest skipped nimbly through. If someone tripped they had to take their turn at "ca'in' the rope". There were many variations and rhymes for the skippers to enter and leave after a specified number of jumps. Boys were meantime playing marbles and the recognised place for the "kypie" was under the school bell tower.

When the skipping season ended - nobody ever knew who decided when - ball games came into their own. All that was needed for most ball games was a ball and a wall to throw it against. Balls often had to be recovered from spouts at Cullen School by a non-too-willing janitor! Again rhymes and jingles were part of the ball play.

At the beginning of many games, rhymes or jingles decided who would be "it", i.e. the child who would be the "seeker" in hide and seek or the one in the centre in circle games. Most of you will remember "eetil ottle black bottle eetil ottle - out" or "one two sky blue all out but - you" and will recall others.

Ball games gave way to hopscotch or beddies on a piece of ground marked out in a squared pattern and played with a piece of slate or small flat stone - costing nothing! In winter, when snow and frost came, children enjoyed making slides and

Playing "bools" in the playground

sledging. The school playground was popular but the more adventurous used to sledge on the streets that were on a slope. There was very little traffic and thus little danger. It was common for children to sledge from the top of Seafield Brae down Seafield Street, past the local bobby standing helpless opposite the burgh cross and right down to the burn! It was a long trail back - but well worth the effort! In summer, boys and girls ran with girds, iron hoops driven and controlled by a piece of stick.

Grown-ups have played golf in Cullen for over 300 years - but only latterly on Sundays! Quoits were played down by the burn at the base of the viaducts. Football, hockey and cricket matches were played on the Links at the far side of the 17th green. Later football and hockey were played on the Glebe.

When the shout "The Lochy's bearing!" went up, it meant that the Crannoch Loch was frozen to a depth sufficient to carry people safely. There could then be skating on frosty days and moonlight nights and also curling on the pond in Cullen House grounds.

Swimming galas used to be held in the harbour for all age groups. Activities included diving for plates and usually the finale was a duck hunt, when a duck was brought from the burn and released in the harbour in front of the expectant youngsters. The duck always escaped and flew away!

Outside bowls have been played in Cullen since the beginning of the century, first on a single green and later on two greens. Tennis was played at one time on six

Today's children learn "hopscotch", a game of yesteryear

blaes courts and they were all full the summer long.

But sadly now none remain. However moves are afoot to restore tennis to Cullen so there's still hope for budding tennis stars. Still on the out-of-doors, people walked more in days gone by - partly of necessity but partly as an activity. Today its amazing the number of inhabitants who confess they have never walked to the top of the Bin Hill. Footpaths which were once widely used are becoming narrower and overgrown through lack of use - for example the path from Logie to Sunnyside.

Indoor activities were many and varied. At one time there were four badminton clubs using the Town Hall, the Drill Hall, the Parish Church Hall and Seafield Church Hall. In post-war years teams played in a keenly contested Coast League. In the Town Hall there was a billiard room and a much-used reading room which was open all day for people to read daily newspapers and periodicals. Apart from games and sports, people could enjoy and participate in many and varied societies, such as the Choral Union, the Literary and Debating Society, the Amateur Dramatic Group and the Townswomen's Guild. Deskford had a Mutual Improvement Association and a Horticultural Society which is still flourishing after 100 years in existence.

By now you will have gathered that over the years we didn't depend on the press of a button for our entertainment. To a large extent we made our own amusement and speaking personally, I don't remember ever in my life suffering from that complaint which is so common these days - that of being bored!

Cullen School Class Four children after a "games of old" session

SOME MEMORIES OF CULLEN TOWN COUNCIL

by Davina Runcie

Davina Runcie has lived all her life in Cullen and has been very much involved in the affairs of the town. Before regionalisation in 1975, she was Depute Town Clerk.

I hope to revive memories of times gone by, when our Royal and Ancient Burgh was economically administered by twelve good men and true, who applied their business acumen to the varied civic duties with no thought of allowances or expenses. They met monthly, sitting at a round table in the round Council chamber within the Town Hall, which was originally built around 1830 by the 7th Earl of Seafield when Cullen was moved from around his mansion. It included a jail and an inn, the present Seafield Arms Hotel. It is on record that around 1900, members of the Town Council used to foregather in the sitting room of the hotel, and restore their strength after working on particularly difficult problems in the Council Chamber; a practice not unknown to be repeated from time to time.

WATER SCHEME - One enterprise which merits highlighting is the Water Scheme. The members in 1932 or thereby, are to be commended for their foresight and courage in embarking on a scheme to acquire the rights of wells and springs at Aultmore and the Grange area to provide us with a constant flow of water, the envy of neighbouring burghs. The cost was over £30,000, a vast sum in those days and was financed by loans from private investors to top up the amount from the Public Works Loan Board. Just when all the borrowing was repaid, and water was costing the Cullen ratepayer next to nothing, the new Water Authority came into being, and the rates for water began to increase annually.

HOUSING - When considering house-building, much thought was always given to design and quality of houses to let - prefabs or Cruden houses were never considered suitable for Cullen but the wooden Swedish houses in Logie Avenue were acceptable, having a longer life and being better value for money. The last development undertaken by the Town Council before its demise was that in Queen's Drive, an ambitious scheme to provide up-market houses for executives. Solid fuel heating was installed, but for some inexplicable reason, the smoke went everywhere except up the lum, and this attracted much adverse publicity. Some Council members even had the dubious honour of being seen on television, defending the indefensible!

Getting the economic rent required proved impossible, and in the end, the houses were offered for sale at £4,700 each, including road and pavement charges.

TOWN OFFICE - It was customary for the local solicitor to be appointed Town Clerk on a part-time basis, operating from his business premises, and thus saving the expense of providing an office. Other officials, the Burgh Surveyor and Town Chamberlain operated from home. However, when the Town Clerk resigned, and a Findochty lawyer was appointed, the Council made available the premises at 16 Reidhaven Street, still in use. This allowed all the Councillors the opportunity to spend more time with the officials. The Provost's lengthy attendance there was noticeable until one morning when the nameplate on the gate of his house was mischievously transferred to the office door!

FREEDOM CEREMONY - When Lewis Bain eventually retired as Provost the Council decided to recognise his lengthy service to the community by giving him the Freedom of the Burgh. At a public ceremony, the scröll was presented to him in a carved oak casket.

TOWN CHAMBERLAIN - The Chamberlain was responsible for financial matters and balancing the books. In this capacity, Miss Margaret Taylor (better known as Meg or Maggie) excelled and created an enviable record of no arrears in rates or housing rents. Every year, a day in November was set aside for the collection of rates in the Council Chambers, with one assistant. She conveniently turned her very deaf ear to anyone complaining, and made a point of emphasising that she herself paid for the morning coffee with hot butteries and lunch brought from the Hotel, as the work had to continue non-stop. She was a formidable figure in a tailored suit, and was never seen without her fawn pudding-shaped hat, summer and winter, the same one it was said, all her life. She trudged from house to house collecting rent and outstanding rates. Her method of recovering arrears was no soft touch, but a real threat of the Sheriff Officer taking away a chiming clock, the wireless and any such luxury her eagle eye spotted. Apart from saving envelopes and stamps by the Burgh Foreman handing over a demand notice to each ratepayer, she was making sure no-one had the excuse that a rates notice had not been delivered.

LINKS - During the summer, fees were collected by the Golf Course Attendant and by the one at the Bathing Shelters - a row of wooden huts beyond the Club House. Deck chairs and wind shields were hired out. Maintenance costs at the

Links were high, as erosion by the sea was a recurring problem. The Links belonged to Lord Reidhaven, and his forebears as Superiors, who granted a long lease to the Council, with no obligation on the Superior to assist in protecting the foreshore. From the Boar Craig to the Bathing Shelters, the Council built a barrier of wooden piles and railway sleepers. In front of this was a considerable bed of shingle, large quantities of which were removed mechanically by building contractors from a wide area, and this aggravated the erosion. The storm of January 1953 swept away the remainder of that barricade. At that time the Links were outwith the Burgh boundary, and the Council did not qualify for Government Grants. Lord Reidhaven gifted the land in 1967 to the Council. This paved the way for extending the Burgh boundary and opened the doors to assistance from Banff County Council and the Government. The Council devoted much thought and effort to protecting the Golf

Cullen golf clubhouse and putting green

Course and was criticised for the burden on the rates to provide sport for a small section of the community, compared with the Bowling Green and Tennis Courts, being privately owned and not affecting the rates. Nowadays the Golf Club shoulders the burden. It is worth mentioning that despite the change of ownership of the land, the rights of fishermen to dry their nets on the Links was continued, but the practice is now outdated. It was a sore point with golfers finding a large fleet of nets spread over the fairways and greens. Needless to say, the fishermen had sometimes reason to complain about damaged nets - not always caused by golfers. Another sore point was the ban on Sunday golf, mainly because the Links had always been the customary walk for families on Sunday. Eventually a compromise was agreed, with restrictions on timing for golfers. At one time, consideration was given to creating a new course on the moor beyond the Crannoch Loch. Acquiring the land alone was too big a hurdle.

BURGH SURVEYOR - The Burgh Surveyor was another official who trudged the streets inspecting work in progress then giving a full written report to the monthly meeting. Fifty years ago there was no central heating. Every household used coal, and put the cinders and ashes into open buckets on the pavement for collection by the horse-drawn wagon. Just picture the scene on a windy day, not to mention the condition of the men who tipped the buckets into the cart. In one report the Burgh Surveyor expressed his wish to see household refuse put out in paper sacks, which only recently came to pass.

Cullen Town Council dust cart around 1940

ELECTION - The first Tuesday of May was a statutory date for the annual election. Shortly beforehand a heckling meeting was held in the Town Hall when candidates and reigning Councillors had to face up to a battery of questions from the ratepayers. Woe betide any candidate who couldn't give some method of reducing the rates. On one occasion someone demanded an explanation for continuing with a recreation project which was not profitable. In reply, the Councillor pointed out all departments could not be gainful and quoted the cemetery as being a dead loss. The heckler was not amused! At the first meeting after the election the Provost and Magistrates were appointed. Usually the previous ones were re-appointed. On one rare occasion two members were proposed as Provost and got equal votes. Normally the Chairman had the casting vote, but this time the Chairman happened to be one of the nominees. The problem was overcome by putting names in a hat. The press reported "Cullen raffles for its Civic Head".

THE HARBOUR - The harbour was another amenity where income and expenditure did not meet. Occasionally a dredger had to be employed to clear the basins. One worthy suggested it would be cheaper to heighten the walls.

TOWN CRIER - When it was necessary to make public announcements, a workman was delegated to act as town crier. Prior to the Water Scheme, spells of drought made it necessary to issue warnings of shortage, and prosecution for wastage. One Crier's version of the message was "Notice, all those found with their water running will have their connections cut off".

Provost Lewis Bain greets the Queen and the Duke of Edinburgh

ROYAL VISIT - A great event which demanded very special organisation was the Royal visit when Her Majesty the Queen and His Royal Highness, the Duke of Edinburgh stopped here for five minutes on 14th August, 1961, arriving at 10.55a.m. and departing at 11.00a.m. The Provost and his wife, the Town Clerk, two Magistrates, the Dean of Guild and the Honorary Treasurer were presented. Instead of having a dais erected at the market cross, the presentation took place at the top of the Town Hall steps. A canopy was erected over the door, a small table set up to take the visitors book, red carpeting laid, lots of pot plants, flowers, flags and bunting. The Girl Guides, the Brownies and other groups were in the forefront. So much preparation for the flash visit, but it created an exciting and memorable day. There had been no Royal Visit since that of King Edward V11 in 1909.

CULLEN WAR MEMORIAL

Cullen's War Memorial in Reidhaven Street, overlooking the Square was unveiled on a cold and dull December day in 1920 by Lieutenant Colonel Dawson D.S.O. in front of 200 ex-servicemen, members of Cullen Town Council, the Parish Council and several other public bodies as well as a large number of citizens.

Col. Dawson was introduced by Captain D. McKenzie M.C. who was a Gordon Highlander Territorial and Headmaster of Cullen School as "one who was great in counsel and great in war", a soldier of distinction who had served with the local battalion of Gordon Highlanders as an officer and as its Commander. He was known to many of those whose names were on the panel of the memorial.

At the end of his address, in which he called for the fallen never to be forgotten Col. Dawson drew aside the Union Jack and read out the names of the 60 who had been killed in action. He concluded with

"Father, in thy tender keeping
Leave me now, Thy servants sleeping".

Pipe-Major Logie of Buckie played a lament and after the benediction, the "Last Post" was sounded on the bugle by C.S.M. Sam Jack of Cullen. The National Anthem was sung and then wreaths were laid by representatives of various organisations.

"CULLEN IN STITCHES"

Hanging in Cullen library, protected by a special ultra-violet perspex cover is a unique wall-hanging which depicts many of the features of Cullen and which will become part of our heritage in future years. The quilted wall-hanging is the result of very many hours of intricate work by the lady members of the Needlework Group who are based at Cullen Community Education Centre.

During 1993 and 1994 members were asked to design and stitch a 'block' of needlework depicting something which represented Cullen to them. A mixture of designs resulted, some depicting local landmarks, some showing the emblems of local clubs and others featuring flora and fauna of the area. One member used a local recipe for the well-known dish Cullen Skink as her theme and another depicted knitwear. Each block was made to a standard size and then they were stitched together around a centrepiece based on the Cullen Coat of Arms.

The final article is a wonderful work of art, encapsulating the skill in design and execution of the art of needlework inherent in the group of Cullen ladies. The quilt, which measures 42" wide by 58" high has been shown at several exhibitions and has attracted much praise for its excellence. It now has justifiably been awarded a place of prominence in Cullen in a showcase specially designed for it by The Moray Council Department of Libraries.

The library keeps a record of all the ladies who contributed to the work and these ladies chose the very appropriate name for the hanging "Cullen in Stitches". They are :- Betsy Addison, Virginia Brook, Margaret Chalmers, Morag Coley, Margaret Donn, Margaret Falconer, Moira Fairbrother, Betty Imlah, Moira Innes, Margaret Kirk, Gladys Leith, Margaret Lownds, Kiturah Martin, Cathie Pirie, Iris Pirie, Karin Rose, Davina Runcie, Margaret Stevenson and Kathleen Turner who also quilted the wall-hanging.

It is well worth a visit to Cullen Library to see the wall-hanging and also to have a look at the fine collection of local books and items of interest which they have there.

RAILWAY TIME

by Bill Davidson

Bill Davidson is a founder member of the Cullen Deskford and Portknockie Heritage Group. For many years he was an electrical contractor in Cullen and also had a business showing films in town and village halls in the days before television. Railways have always been one of his interests. He now lives in retirement in sheltered housing in Cullen.

Before the advent of railways in 1825, there was very little chance of two towns having the same time on their clocks. There could be as much difference as 10 or 15 minutes between two neighbouring towns, there being no regular means of conveying one town's time to another. Thus a person who had travelled on foot or by horse from Portsoy and was in good time according to his (Portsoy) time for an appointment with someone in Cullen could be late if his host was using Cullen time!

In London in 1825 a lady with a horse and gig went to Greenwich every morning, set her watch to the Observatory time and then went round all the public clocks giving them the correct time. For this service she received a payment. In the country the guards on the stage coaches often carried watches and ran to a time table, not very accurate but enough for farmers and others along the road to set their

The afternoon mail train from Inverness crossing Cullen viaducts in 1945

watches or judge the time when the coach went by.

When towns and villages were connected by the railways, the guards each carried fairly accurate watches and it was part of their duties to check and set the clock at each station as they passed along the line. From 1850 the railways covered much of the country, as far north as Aberdeen and beyond so a reasonably consistent time was established.

When the telegraph was invented in 1870, the railway companies quickly set up the new system throughout their networks to improve communications. They set up poles alongside their tracks and using the recently invented morse code, were able to communicate between stations.

It is interesting to record that prior to the telegraph, on single tracks there was a "staff" system to prevent two trains being on the same length of line. The driver received the staff from the dispatching end and carried it to the next signalbox. On receipt of the staff the signalman could allow a train going in the opposite direction to occupy the line and take back the staff.

A major difficulty was that if there was no returning train, another could not proceed unless someone walked or cycled back with the token. When the two signal boxes were in communication with one another by telegraph, an improved token system allowed one train to follow another over the same track with the co-operation of both signalmen.

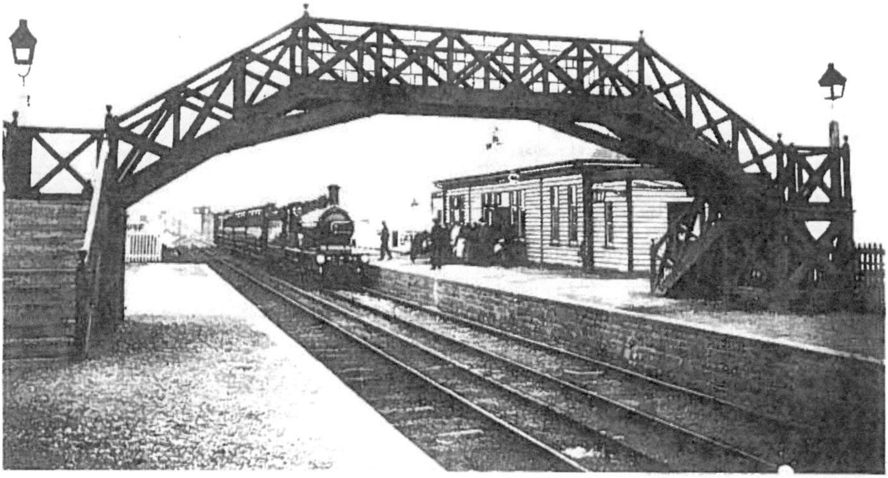

Train standing at Portknockie Station

The Post Office were quick to use the railway telegraph system and put their lines on the poles already in existence along the railway tracks to save the cost of a new system along the highways. With post offices and stations now all interconnected, this was an opportunity to set a common time throughout the whole country. At two minutes to ten every morning all telegraph business ceased, all operators stood by their telegraphs until on the dot of 10 o'clock a signal was sent from Greenwich. Thus all railway and post office clocks were synchronised at what was called Railway Time.

Watchmakers in towns and villages would go to the station before 10 o'clock to set their own watches and they then went round setting the public and other clocks in "big houses", Town Halls and such. This use of "railway time" continued until the advent of broadcasting in the twenties when the "Greenwich Time Signal" was broadcast regularly and Greenwich Time was universally used throughout the country and still is today.

THE FAMOUS CULLEN VIADUCTS

When the Coast Line between Cairnie Junction and Elgin was proposed, the then Earl and Countess of Seafield refused to let the railway cross the policies of Cullen House and as a result high embankments and brick and masonry arches had to be built. They have come to be known as the Cullen Viaducts and are world famous. They give a special air to the town and provide a "frame" for some fine views of Cullen Bay and of the town itself. In the days before the railway closed, crossing the viaducts and enjoying the view was the biggest thrill of the coast line.

Completed for the opening of the line in 1886, the viaducts were in service until the line was closed in 1968. They are now "monuments" in the care of the Moray Council and despite their age are in remarkably good condition.

They are a fine example of Victorian engineering and a very considerable asset to Cullen and must be preserved. Some day, when the Cullen by-pass road is built somewhere to the south of the town the viaducts will still have their proud place as a feature of Cullen.

THE POWER OF THE DESKFORD BURN

by Len Hall

Len Hall is a retired engineer and lecturer. He became co-ordinator of the Cullen Deskford and Portknockie Heritage Group when it was founded seven years ago and heritage is now his main hobby along with writing.

Many songs, stories and poems have been written in praise of many of the world's great rivers - the Blue Danube, old man Mississippi, and old Father Thames are examples. Now is the time to redress the balance and put on record the important part that the Deskford Burn has played in the life of the Deskford/Cullen area in years past. The burn is called the Deskford burn until it enters the policies of Cullen House when officially or otherwise it becomes the Cullen burn.

The burn starts its life in the Aultmore and Lurg hills at a height of about 1000 feet and travels six miles before it discharges into the sea at Cullen Beach. It flows gently down the Deskford Valley, mostly through rich farmland growing in size and strength as it collects water draining off the hills and fields. This little jingle (origin unknown) names many of the farms it passes.

Clochmacreich and Langlanburn
Craibstone and Raemore
Burnheads and Squaredoch
Mosside and Ardoch
Nether Blairoch and The Clune
Are passed as it weirs its wey doon.

Although today it travels to the sea almost without hindrance, this was not always so and for many years it had to work hard for its passage to the sea. The first major work done by the burn was at Craibstone where for 100 years up to the second world war, it fed a substantial dam which in turn drove a large water-wheel to drive machinery. Limestone was quarried, crushed, burnt, finely ground and bagged for agricultural purposes and the building industry. Although it is fast disappearing back to nature, much can still be seen of the workings which were the subject of a study by members of the Scottish Vernacular Buildings Working Group in 1995.

After a peaceful run for a mile or two, the water of the burn was gathered in two dams and used to drive a water-wheel at Berryhillock Mill where corn was dried and milled to make oatmeal. The mill, like the village of Berryhillock dates from about 1800 and was noted for having millstones of French Burr, the only mill of its kind in the district. Another feature of the mill was a figure of a horse on top of its

Berryhillock Mill in its prime

pagoda-like louvred top. The mill was closed for good in 1965 and the dams filled in. The burn meanders through what was once an orchard, popular at one time as a place for Sunday School picnics but now used as a scout camp-site. Then it was back to work, another dam, a lade, a wheel and more corn to grind at Milton Mills until it closed in the 1950's.

Until the 1930's, the burn helped in the manufacture of linen at Bleachfield. Besides driving a wheel to power the mill machinery, water was fed along canals for washing the cloth to remove the alkalis and acids used in the bleaching process. (never let it be said that pollution of rivers is something new). Washing, along with bleaching and drying occupied about 10 acres of flat ground near the burn.

As it approached Tochieneal, the burn encountered intense activity. It was harnessed again to grind corn at the Mill of Towie which dates back to 1668. Next it helped to make bricks, tiles, drain pipes and flower pots at the Tochineal Brick and Tile Works and this lasted until the days of the second world war. Some, but very little evidence can be seen of the dams and lades associated with these activities.

From about 1820, the water of the Deskford Burn was used via a water wheel to drive the machinery at Tochieneal Distillery. But in 1870, partly due to the poor quality of the water and partly due to a disagreement with the Countess of Seafield, the entire distillery was moved to Inchgower near Buckie. This was a sad loss to Tochieneal - sad also that the world was deprived of a good dram of "Old Tochieneal". In earlier days, in the 18th century, the Earl of Seafield started a mill to speed up the flax processing operation and this mill was powered from a dam back at the Mill of Towie. Unfortunately the mill, which may have had as many as 65 looms did not prosper.

Downstream from Lintmill bridge, the burn fed a large dam which drove a water wheel to provide power for a sawmill operated by Seafield Estates. Later this was replaced with a steam engine and about twenty years ago a new electrically powered sawmill was installed in Lintmill. Within the Estate, in the vicinity of Cullen House, the burn performs decorative and sporting functions only and despises work. As it winds its way through the gorge, it blends into the garden scheme and further down the attractively formed pools provide good fishing.

There is some written evidence however, that in earlier times there was another corn mill, a waulk mill for pounding linen, a snuff mill and a tannery somewhere in the lower reaches of the burn but of these nothing can be seen today. Finally the burn passes under the road, rail and foot bridges to discharge into the sea at Seatown. But that it still possesses its ample powers was demonstrated in 1995 when during a spate, it gouged a deep, wide and straight channel for itself right down to bedrock through the shingle from the viaduct down to the sea! It was an impressive bit of natural engineering, amply demonstrating the power of natural forces!

The Deskford Carnyx

In 1816 a farm labourer was digging a trench deep down in a peat bog on the farm of Leitchieston in Deskford. The labourer came upon an oddly shaped bronze object, shaped like a boar's head. This was taken to the National Museum in Edinburgh and a replica left in Banff. In 1950 it was recognised as the head of a Carnyx, a Pictish war horn about 2000 years old and one of the best examples ever found in Europe. A replica of the complete war trumpet was made by a team of highly skilled technicians and musicians and in 1993 the wild and haunting sound of the Carnyx was heard in the Deskford Valley after many centuries. In 1994 a team of archaeologists from Edinburgh started a "dig" in the area and found enough evidence of early life to justify two more visits. It is fascinating to think that early man lived in Deskford.

LOCAL "GIRL PAT" CONNECTIONS

by Arnold Pirie

Arnold Pirie is a retired policeman who has served in several stations in the north-east of Scotland as well as in England. Originally from Portsoy, he now lives in Portknockie and his hobbies are music, sea-fishing from his small boat and researching local heritage.

A few years ago at a meeting of the Cullen Deskford and Portknockie Heritage Group, I was invited to research the local connection with an event which took place in 1936. A Grimsby trawler was stolen by a man brought up in Deskford. With his brother as crew and a young lad as cook, he sailed it across the Atlantic, disappearing in the process and giving rise to a sea and air search which made world headlines. Little did I know where my research would lead me and the story is told here as an example of just how interesting heritage can be.

The basic facts are that on 1 April 1936 the 75 foot Grimsby trawler named the "Girl Pat" registered number GY176 left her home port under the command of Skipper George (Dod) Orsborne with five of a crew, ostensibly for a fishing trip in the North Sea. Instead of heading for the fishing grounds, for a reason which has never really been understood, Skipper Orsborne headed for the English Channel, dropped off one crew member at Dover, then sailed across the Bay of Biscay to Corcubion in Spain. After a stay of 14 days the merry adventurers headed south towards Africa and the Canary Islands, eventually landing on Tenerife for a short stay before moving down the African coast, calling at various ports, getting stuck on a sand bank and eventually reaching Dakar. Here another crew member decided to stay ashore and despite being warned by officials not to sail, Skipper Orsborne and his now depleted crew headed westward to cross the Atlantic, navigating as he had done since leaving Grimsby with the aid of a sixpenny schoolboy atlas. They made land off Georgetown in British Guyana. Details of his adventures, his attempts to disguise the boat, the final chase, the arrest, conviction and sentence are not for this story - sufficient to say that the adventure caught the imagination of the world's press. Aeroplanes and ships searched for the "Girl Pat" and her crew and it made a wonderful diversion at a time when the world was in sore need of some "light relief".

Our local interest stems from the fact that the two main characters in the story, Skipper 'Dod' Orsborne and his brother Jim had been brought up by foster parents in Kirktown, Deskford and had attended Deskford School. In the newspaper reports of the time it was said that their father was George Black, a resident of the Seatown of Buckie. Their mother remarried and took the name Orsborne. At the time of his escapade 'Dod' lived in Grimsby and was married with three children. Brother Jim had recently returned from Canada. After their arrest in Georgetown on charges connected with the "Girl Pat", their adventures continued because while on bail in Georgetown awaiting return to Britain it appears they were again arrested for fighting and causing damage in a restaurant! Apparently their desire for mischief was insatiable! On their return to Britain, Skipper Orsborne was sentenced at the Old Bailey London to 18 months hard labour for offences concerning the "Girl Pat" and James Orsborne to 12 months.

While their adventure with somebody else's boat amounted to theft and caused much trouble and cost to the authorities and others, it provided a good story for the media at a time when there was little else happening except gathering clouds of war. It was a considerable feat to have sailed across the Atlantic without charts, using a sixpenny atlas and it certainly caught the imagination of the public. Was Skipper Orsborne forgiven or did he redeem himself? It is believed he served his country well during the 1939-45 war as Lieutenant Commander in the Royal Navy. He died in 1957 of a heart attack in France. The only member of the crew still alive is Howard Stephen who was the 17 year old cook on the Girl Pat. He was also born in Buckie and before moving to Grimsby had lived with his grandmother Mrs Stephen at 14 Bridgend Buckie and been fostered with a Miss Kate Donald at Berryhillock Deskford. He attended Deskford School for five years and then worked for a local farmer Mr John Morrison at Ordens Deskford before moving to Grimsby. My enquiries have traced Mr Stephen to his home at Bethel, St. Austel, Cornwall and I have been in regular communication with him by letter, telephone and tape. Howard paid a visit to Deskford and made contact with the late Mrs Nett Weakley of Upper Darbreich, Deskford who knew him when he lived in Deskford. Now in his late seventies, Howard still remembers the exploit with something approaching nostalgia.

The final and perhaps the most interesting link with the "Girl Pat" is the fact that I made acquaintance with Roy Skinner of Ellon, a retired engineer in his nineties who died a few years ago. Roy, a very alert and active man came into the story because he was the man who overhauled the engine of the "Girl Pat" to enable it to be sailed home to Britain. He was employed at the time on a sugar plantation near Georgetown and in the course of working in the engine room found a pair of binoculars which he believed belonged to the boat or to Skipper Orsborne. He was given permission to keep them and still had them at the time of his death. The accompanying photograph shows Roy Skinner outside my house in Portknockie with the binoculars he found on the Girl Pat in 1936.

Roy Skinner (centre) with the binoculars he found on the "Girl Pat"

As for the "Girl Pat" herself, she was brought back to this country by a company who put her on show round the ports of Britain on a "pay to see" basis. Because of her fame many people saw over her and by the time interest faded, it was time for her to go to war as a minesweeper. After the war it is believed she worked on the River Thames for the Port of London Authority and unconfirmed reports have her being used as a ferry at the Island of Rhodes in the 1970's. For a humble fishing boat she had an exciting life.

Nobody knows what possessed Skipper Orsborne to steal his boat, to give himself a criminal record and to risk his own and his crew's life in such a mad adventure. Was it boredom? Did he do it on a mad impulse? In the end they were lucky to get away with their lives. Isn't it funny how a relatively insignificant incident caught the public imagination and is still remembered today as a bit of our history. The children of the time in Grimsby sang this song to the tune "Red sails in the Sunset" -

The Girl Pat left Grimsby, to sail the north Sea,
Now everyone's wondering where she could be.
She was heard of in Dover, then landed in Spain,
And now Skipper Orsborne has vanished again.
Swift wings he must borrow, keep away from the shore,
If they catch you tomorrow, then you'll be Skipper no more!

DESKFORD NOW AND AS IT WAS 65 YEARS AGO

By William Smith

William Smith took over the farm of Braidbog on the south side of the Bin Hill from his father in 1943 and farmed it until 1963 when he moved to Cullen to run a confectionery business. He later became an agricultural representative and maintains a great interest in the well-being of farming. Here he tells of the changes which have taken place in Deskford during his lifetime.

In 1930 there were two meal mills, one at Berryhillock and one at Milton, employing four men in all. There were also two smiddies, one at Cottarton employing four men, and one at Berryhillock employing three men and believe me they were kept busy. There were two shoemakers, one in the village of Kirktown employing two men repairing and making shoes, while in nearby Berryhillock there was a cobbler who concentrated on repairing boots and shoes for farmers and farm workers. There were three shops in all, two in Berryhillock (one with the Post Office) and one in Kirktown which more or less sold everything that the people in the parish required.

There was also a lime kiln at Craibstone where the lime produced was famed far beyond Deskford for its quality both for building and application to the land. The fact that good quality lime was readily available locally probably accounts for the high state of fertility of the farms in the vicinity.

Two churches looked after the spiritual needs of the parishioners. The old Established Church was situated on the main roadside near the school while the United Free Church was one half mile to the north west, both having large congregations in those days.

The school had a headmaster and three qualified teachers with approximately 150 pupils. The ministers and teachers were instrumental in organising most of the social life in the parish which included The Mutual Improvement Association, The Ladies Guilds, Amateur Dramatics Club, Badminton Club and a Quoiting Club. There was also a Football Club which perhaps did not benefit from the help of the Ministers and teachers - as I remember it, if you could fight you were sure of a place in the team!

The ruins of three Castles, at Inaltrie, at Kirktown and at Mains of Skeith could be seen sixty years ago but today only those at Kirktown and Inaltrie can be seen. The stones from these castles have in all probability been incorporated in various farm buildings. All the land at Deskford belonged to the Earl of Seafield and

Harvest scene in the days of the horse-drawn binder

was rented out to farmers and crofters. The rent for a good farm in the valley was approximately £1 per acre, for one slightly higher up 15 shillings while for crofts and holdings well up the hill on both sides of the valley the rent was 10 shillings per acre. The Seafield Estates were very good landlords and maintained the houses and steadings well above average for the period. By the sixties rents had doubled and they continued to rise so that at the present day £35 per acre is normal.

Now as to the wages paid to farm workers, I am fortunate in having access to records kept by my late mother's uncle, who farmed Kirktown Farm and which date back to 1845. For example, in 1845 he paid his first horseman £7:10/-, his cattleman £2:5/-. and his servant girl £1:5/-, all for six months work and keep. By 1900 these rates had risen to £15 for the first horseman, £12 for the cattleman and £7 for the servant girl whilst in 1931 a first horseman would have been getting £21, a cattleman £15 and a servant girl £10.

The "keep" or board and lodgings provided varied from farm to farm, sometimes good but quite often just above bare subsistence and were often the reason for servants moving on from one place to another. It was said that if a place was bad, then the next one could only be better and if a place was good, somebody else would get the good of it when you moved.

Up to the Second World War there were what was known as "feeing markets" twice yearly, on the 28th May and 28th November where farmers and workers concluded their bargain for six month's employment. Married men in cottar houses were on a yearly basis. Many of them settled for only one year on any one farm. After the second World War the whole system changed and farm workers were employed and paid weekly. Between 1950 and the early sixties, the average wage was £10.00 per week whereas today I understand the weekly wage is at least £200.00. Up to the second war workers were working a 60 hour week with no holidays but now the working week has been reduced to 44 hours with three weeks holidays

In 1930 there were only three tractors in the whole of Deskford. All the work was done with horses and any work which could not be done with horses had to be done by hand - sheer hard graft! Another highlight in the working of a farm before the second world war was the "road mill" or the "steam mull" as it was known locally, used for threshing grain on the farm. A steam traction engine (later replaced by a tractor) pulled the mill and the small crew which travelled with the mill either

A "TITAN" tractor at work in the fields many years ago

stayed in the caravan towed behind the mill or got lodgings at the farm. It required 16 to 20 men to operate the mill and neighbouring farmers supplied this labour on a reciprocal basis. This meant a very busy few days for the farmer's wife as a mountain of oatcakes had to be baked and huge pots of soup, meat and potatoes and milk puddings prepared. All this disappeared in minutes when the men sat down to eat.

Fertiliser arrived at the farm in 12 stone bags and when grain was sold off the farm, oats were in 12 stone bags, barley 16 stone, and wheat (where grown) was put in 18 stone bags. Material packaged in these weights had to be manhandled so you had to be pretty fit to do a day's work, handling bags up and down loft stairs. At the present time fertiliser comes in a variety of large packages which are handled by machines, such as fork lift trucks. The law nowadays does not allow anyone to lift more than 4 or 5 stones. Grain is all handled in bulk and loaded by elevators into bins or tankers - a vast improvement. Where the loading of dung, etc. was all done by hand using a graip, it is all now done by tractor loaders. A tractor driver now has seldom to leave his seat in a nicely heated cab, soundproofed and as often as not equipped with radio and telephone. Prices for fat cattle have changed dramatically over the years. A fat bullock in 1850 fetched approximately £20 and the price remained pretty constant throughout the thirties. But by 1960 a bullock would have fetched at least £65 and today it would be worth over £700.

Grain prices in the thirties were £5 per ton for oats, £7 for barley and by the sixties these had risen to £15 and £20 respectively. Today oats and barley are worth £110 to £120 per ton and wheat, which has become much more popular is also priced at £120. Yield per acre has increased tremendously and whereas one ton per acre was common in the sixties, the extensive use of better fertilisers and the higher yielding types of seed has raised the average yield to 2 tons per acre.

Probably the biggest change to have taken place in Deskford as in most other areas is the amalgamation of small farms and crofts into larger units and there are only a few small farms left. One day recently I sat on the top of the Bin Hill and counted 23 farms and crofts from which families had attended Deskford School. Now all are farmed as one unit. They are not all empty and abandoned for some have been renovated and are owned by people who have no direct connection with agriculture but overall the population has dramatically decreased.

Another change is in the postal service. In the thirties two postmen on bicycles delivered all mail from Cullen, providing a pretty regular service and on time except on Tuesdays when the "Banffies" were delivered. Very few farmers got a daily paper in those days but now they have at least one delivered by a postman in a van from the nearby town of Buckie.

In the north of Deskford prior to 1923 there were tremendous forests around the Bin Hill area and very heavy timber of exceptional quality was felled and processed by George Auld and Sons who had a sawmill installed at Braidbog. There was also a railway system to assist extraction, comprising horse-drawn bogies on a narrow gauge track all the way along the High Glen. At a point below the sawmill the bogies were transferred to another track to be hauled up the steep hill by a steel rope powered by the steam engine which drove the sawmill. Roughly 20 men were employed at the forestry until in 1929 the sawmill was moved to Burnlevnit on the edge of the Hill of Maud. Later, in 1930 it was re-sited at Woodside and the whole area around the Bin was felled and replanted. The sawn timber was transported to Aberdeen by a Sentinel steam lorry with solid rubber tyres.

In this paper I have tried to record the big changes which have occurred in the course of a lifetime in a rural area which was and is almost entirely dependent on agriculture and to a lesser extent on forestry. It is not part of my remit to say whether all the changes have been for the better but though times have changed, the folks of Deskford are still the salt of the earth, industrious and warm-hearted. Despite the countryside being less densely populated, all the country shops closed, the local school gone and the kirk operating on a part-time basis, the spirit of the rural community is still there. There is a very thriving Deskford and District Community Association which is responsible for running the Community Centre which was the former school. A vast amount of work was done to raise money to pay for the conversion and now twenty years after it is still being maintained by the Community in first class order. It is extensively used for youth clubs, bowling, badminton as well as for dances, Burns Suppers and such like. The Deskford Horticultural Society which has been in existence for over 100 years, is still flourishing and holds its popular show every year in August. The Deskford Mutual Improvement Society may have passed into history but its spirit lives on. Deskford has not died as the result of the changes but change it certainly has.

Dr WILLIAM CRAMOND

William Cramond was Headmaster of Cullen School from 1871 until 1904. It was a time of great change in Scottish education, when the control of schools passed into the hands of School Boards. In 1876 the school was moved to a new building (now the Community Centre) in Seafield Street. Dr Cramond was a man of vision and introduced many revolutionary concepts into education. His school log books provide much information about the problems of teaching in those days. He was a noted historian and wrote 60 books, the most notable being "The Annals of Cullen". In 1892 the Senatus of Aberdeen University awarded him an Honorary Doctorate for his historical researches and writings.

THE STORY OF CULLEN HARBOUR

by David Mair and James George Addison

David Mair is a Cullen man who now lives in Portknockie. He has had a lifetime interest in boats and all things maritime and in retirement continues his interest by researching into the history of fishing in this area. James George Addison, also a Cullen man has the same interests and has amassed a considerable collection of photographs connected with the area .

As far back as 1619 there was a "decayit herberie" in Cullen, probably a crude bulwark erection which was prone to storm damage and too small for large vessels. In those days Cullen's fishermen were known as "the seamen under the hill", being crofters who had been evicted from Old Cullen in 1613 by Sir Walter Ogilvy of Findlater to start a fishing industry.

Despite the Earl of Findlater having commissioned plans for a harbour in 1736, Cullen still had no harbour in 1792 when it was described as "the place where the fisher boats are hauled ashore". But in 1819 Colonel Grant got the project under way by "laying out £4000 sterling for the erection of a harbour". He had arranged for one half to be paid by his brother the Earl of Seafield and the other half by the Commissioners for Highland Roads and Bridges. By 1825 there were 14 boats in Seatown and in 1834 the harbour was greatly enlarged and an additional quay built

Cullen Harbour around the turn of the century

so that it became "one of the best harbours in the Moray Firth". In 1841 harbour dues were 2d per ton and the annual revenue was £70. A new era began in 1883 when a Board of Management took over control of the harbour from the Town Council and the Earl of Seafield. Money for repairs to storm damage and for improvements came from fund-raising bazaars as well as from the Fishery Board and from the Countess of Seafield. In 1901, and at the peak of the fishing prosperity 79 boats were based at Cullen. By 1914 the harbour had reached its present state, one of the last major changes being the removal of Paterson's farm and its rebuilding at Blantyre. But fishing was in decline and by 1920 the number of drifters had fallen to 27. Minor improvements continued - a new lifeboat was purchased in 1924 to safeguard bathers on the beach and the harbour light was installed in 1931 at a cost of £62.

By the start of the war in 1939 there were only 9 drifters based in Cullen and most of these went to war, fishing virtually ceased and Cullen Harbour went on a war footing. Nets were laid in the bay, concrete anti-tank blocks built along the links, a minefield laid at the west side and two large gun positions built at the Golf Club to cover the beach should a landing be attempted. In addition several machine gun posts were built, three flame throwers installed to cover vital parts of the harbour, poles erected on the beach to foil aircraft landings and anti-tank ditches dug. High concrete barriers were built on the north and west piers and provision was made to block the jetty by steel poles.

A corner of Cullen Harbour in busy fishing days

An old motorised Fifie filled with stones was kept in readiness to be sunk in the entrance should the need arise, in place of a steel floating boom which did not prove satisfactory. Thankfully none of these precautions were needed but sadly none of the drifters returned to Cullen after the war.

Ship-building has been carried out to a limited extent in Cullen over the years, notably at the east side of the harbour. An attempt to restart boatbuilding after the war was made but all hopes disappeared when the last yard, commonly known as the Black Shed was destroyed with all its contents during the Great Gale of 1953. Over the years small industries supporting fishing such as rope-making, curing and net-preserving yards have existed mainly on the east side of the harbour but with the decline of the fishing these have disappeared and today Cullen's "herberie" is given over almost entirely to a few lobster boats and pleasure craft.

The following lines were penned by Mrs Lily Boyd (nee Mair) who now lives in Canada. Mrs Boyd is a niece of Mrs Elsie Stewart of Cullen who arranged for permission to include the poem about Cullen Harbour then and now.

"Faur are the boats that filled the herbour
A' gittin' ready tae sail wi' the tide?
The Diligent, the Tyrie, the Flower o' May,
The Christmas Morn, the Sunnyside?

Faur's the pier that wis black wi men
An' larries an' ropes an' gear?
As the boats made ready anither time
An' hoped for a better year.

Faur are the loons that swing on the ropes
An' the quines that hoped they'd fa'?
An' the tarry smell of barkit nets
An' the heat o' the sun ower a'?

While doon on the sannies the bairnies played
Diggin' their hoosies an' rinnin' aboot
Fechtin' an' greein' an' widen' an' dookin'
Free as the gulls since the school cam' oot.

Up on the rocks their mithers sat wyvin'
Pins in their wiskers flashin' like licht
Gansies an' drawers an' sea boot stockin's
Tae keep their men warm on a North Sea nicht.

Noo the men are gone an' the boats are gone,
Awa' tae their last lang rest
An' the herbour's quaet an' silted up
A swimmin' pool at best.

For the herrin' left an' the winter came
An' the wind blew sharp an' caul'
An' the bonny loons an' the lauchin' quines
Weel they've a' groun aul'.

But tho' there's jist sma' boaties noo
Ye'll still see bairnies play
Still diggin' hoosies in the sands
Through the lang lang simmer's day"

A CULLEN CARTER'S TALE

Nearly everyone will have heard the Aberdeen story of the carter's horse which dropped down dead in Constitution Street, down near the Beach Boulevard. The bobby who came on the scene was fresh in from the country and was better endowed physically than mentally. After struggling for some time with his notebook and pencil stub, he said to the carter "Come on min - gie's a han' tae pull the puir beast intae Park Sreet - its easier tae spell".

The Cullen equivalent story concerns another dead horse. In the old days there was a lot of horse-drawn carting between the station and the harbour, coal being one of the main commodities. One day a coalman's horse collapsed and died in the middle of the street under the viaduct at the foot of Seafield Street. A rather officious young bobby, anxious to do everything according to the letter of the law asked the carter if he knew why the horse had died. "Fegs, I dinna ken, constable - it's niver deen 'is afore in a' its life"!

THE CULLEN MAIN DRAIN

by Len Hall

William Smith, a former member of the Group discovered an article about the Main Drain in the Banffshire Journal of the period and this provided much of the technical information for this article. It is interesting to note that although provision was made on the original carving of the commemorative plaque for the cost to be stated, for some reason it was not done. The photograph is by another group member Bill Davidson.

Cullen is famous for the railway viaducts which are a very prominent feature of the town and which are a fine example of Victorian railway engineering, bold in concept, clever in construction and built to last. The viaducts were built for the opening in 1886 of the coast line from Tochieneal towards Elgin because the Countess of Seafield did not want the railway to go through the grounds of Cullen House. But the working life of the viaducts was a mere 82 years before the Beeching cuts rendered them useless and left them with an uncertain long-term future.

By contrast, within a few miles of the viaduct is another marvel of Victorian engineering which is still doing the job for which it was designed, unspectacularly and away from the public gaze after 130 years of faithful service. This is the man-made waterway known as the "Main Drain", nearly two and a half miles long which runs within Seafield Estates ground, starting at Rannas to the west and finishing at Claypots where it discharges into the Cullen Burn. It was built by John Charles, Earl of Seafield about 20 years before the railway came and its purpose was to drain the bog area which lay between the Bin Hill and what is now the main road between Cullen and Buckie.

The area, about three miles long by a mile wide was once a loch called the Bin Loch and has been transformed over the years into fertile arable land. It is bounded at its east end by a sand and gravel bank and at some time in the distant past the loch must have broken through and escaped to the sea, leaving a marshy bog. For many years the citizens of Cullen had the right, granted by the Earl of Seafield, to gather peat from the moss as their main source of fuel. It is said that several trunks of black oak and the remains of pines were found deep in the substrata, indicating that different forests had grown and died over the millions of years.

This peat plays quite an important part in the history of Cullen. Coal was becoming available as an alternative fuel to peat at a price which ordinary people could afford but it had to be imported at Portsoy as this was the only harbour in the area capable of handling coal ships. In 1817 the Earl of Seafield decided to build an improved harbour at Cullen to increase trade, encourage fishing and to allow coal to be imported. As a result he was able to withdraw from the citizens of Cullen the right to gather fuel from the Rannas peat bogs. The Earl was thus able to make a start at draining the bog and to make the ground arable. At that time there was an increasing demand for agricultural products, food, wool, leather etc. to meet the demands of the growing population. It was a good long-term investment to recover the land for farming and a start was made by digging a ditch and cutting a tunnel through the sand bank, but as the water drained away the ground sunk and it was decided that a more permanent drainage system was needed to give the scheme a long term future.

Over the next six years, from August 1859 until November 1865 a carefully graded and soundly engineered drain was built, comprising 2505 yards of open drain and 1680 yards of tunnel through the gravel bank. This gathered the water from a system of field drains and conveyed it to the Cullen Burn and then to the sea. Its careful grading and quality of construction ensured even flow with minimum silting or flooding and the effective design and construction is demonstrated by the fact that it has lasted until today without major reconstruction and with minimum maintenance.

For its time the drain was a major work, comparable in many ways with building a railway but at a higher cost per mile. Steam power was available but much of the work was done by hand and materials transported by horse and cart, giving employment for thirty to forty men. Almost all the material used was obtained locally. A quarry was opened on the side of the Bin Hill and stones were brought from the shore at Portlong, east of Cullen. All the timber came from Seafield Estates and only the best was used. This is borne out by the fact that the bottom timbers are still as fresh as the day they were placed in position.

Along the length of the drain, logs cut from home-grown pine were driven into the sub-soil at intervals on either side, and after the tops were levelled, sleepers were laid lengthways and nailed down. The space between was filled with heavy rough stones and this foundation was overlain crossways with planks, seven feet long by three inches thick, laid as close as possible to one another. On these planks were built the side walls of stone and lime to the height of two and a half feet and three feet apart. The stone walls were capped with bricks to a distance of two feet beyond the edge. Beyond that the ground was grassed and sloped at 40 degrees to prevent loose earth falling into the drain.

Towards the east of the works, the depth of the cutting was more than twenty feet deep and tunnelling was adopted instead of open cutting. The tunnel was also three feet wide at its base and was built in whinstone with an arch height of five feet. Every hundred yards along its length manholes were built to the surface two feet square to give access to clear obstructions and avoid water build-up. Beyond the tunnel end the drain reverts to open channel, joining the Cullen Burn at Claypots after cascading over a series of flat steps, six inches deep. Where it enters the burn the drain widens to an impressive seven feet. At the eastern end of the tunnel, on the ornamental granite and freestone facing is a handsome plaque, giving details of the drain (except for its cost) and credits for its construction. It says -

> "This main drain, constructed by John Charles, Earl of Seafield at an expense of £ under the superintendence of W G Bryson, Factor; Francis Currie, Engineer and Overseer. Commenced August 1859, finished November 1865."
> Length of conduit 1680 yds of open drain 2505 yds
> Greatest depth of cutting 20 feet

This perhaps is an inadequate memorial to the instigators, the engineer and the men who laboured over many years to construct a minor engineering marvel. The end of the railway viaduct and the end of the drain are only a few hundred yards apart. One stands proud but useless, the other hides itself but still works well after 130 years of doing the job for which it was designed.

Plaque on the end face wall of the tunnel commemorating the construction of the drain

THE NIGHT THE WARPLANE DITCHED IN CULLEN BAY

by Alex. Mowat

Alex. Mowat is a Cullen man who now lives in Findochty and at the beginning of the war he was a joiner working for Willie Jaffrey in South Deskford Street Cullen. He recalls the night he was involved in a rescue when one of our aeroplanes landed on the sea in Cullen Bay when returning from a bombing mission.

My father Joe Mowat had a motor boat called the Quest. It was one of the kind we called Baldys and there were about a dozen of them in Cullen at that time belonging to local fishermen. They used to fish in the Firth and come back to Cullen in the evenings. At that time I worked with Willie Jaffrey of Cullen as a joiner and I usually took a walk down to the harbour to see my father and the other fishermen after my tea.

In November 1939 I was at the top of the Skemmels Brae when I heard a siren

Seatown, Cullen around the time of the Second World War showing Staples rocks on the left of picture

out in the bay but I could see nothing as there were no street lights and everywhere was pitch dark. I ran down to our house at the Seatown to tell my father and two brothers John and Joe, who were just finishing their meal, that I thought there was a plane down in the bay near the Staples, the rocks at the mouth of the burn. We ran down to the harbour and got the boat under way. When we reached the plane we did not know whether it was British or German until the first man, who was standing on the wing came on board. He said "Thank God I'm not a sailor!". It was then we knew it was a British plane.

When we got the crew (I think there were five of them) back to the harbour the policeman got a car and took them to Doctor Wood's surgery in Reidhaven Street. The pilot was the only one who was injured. We took the boat out again and towed the plane, an Avro Anson, into the harbour. The wing span was too wide to get it into the channel so we had to take it in side on. We pulled it towards the east beach at the harbour. By this time most of the people who lived in the Seatown were down to see what was going on. Then the policeman came down and got everyone away from the harbour as the pilot had told them that there was a bomb jammed in the undercarriage of the plane. The policeman asked my brother Joe to get a small boat from the inner basin to take him out to the plane to get the pilot's log and papers. Joe went on to the plane and got all the papers and the log book and handed them to the police. Within a few days, mechanics from Lossiemouth aerodrome dismantled the wings and took the plane away by road. We were told that the plane had been out bombing German ships and bases in Norway and was returning to its base at Lossiemouth.

A FAMOUS CULLEN STORY

In the days when Cullen had its own gasworks, it was customary for gentlemen from the outlying places who had over-indulged in Cullen's hostelries and were experiencing difficulty in making their way home to seek refuge overnight in the furnace room. There they were assured of warmth while they slept off the effects of their excesses and perhaps get a reviving cup of tea before they set off for home in the morning.

The story goes that one "guest", on waking in the wee sma' hoors saw the stoker shovelling coal into the open door of the furnace and thought he was in Hell. The stoker, noticing that he was awake bade him "good morning" and asked him where he came from. He received the astonishing reply "Well Sir, fan' I wis in the ither warld, I bade in Deskart".

THE HAY FAMILY AND RANNAS HOUSE

by Alan Burgess

Alan Burgess hails from near Liverpool and came to live on a croft on the Hill of Maud about 20 years ago. He has a special interest in the history of the area in which he lives, not far from Rannas House.

A few miles to the west of Cullen, within the Seafield Estates policies are to be found the last vestiges of a family which has an interesting history and which had a considerable influence on events about 250 years ago. Nestling on the north edge of the Bin of Cullen lies the derelict property known as Rannas House and its associated farm buildings. There are in fact two houses at Rannas, one quite a lot older than the other and built in a rather unusual manner in that one is a mirror image of the other. They are separated by a quadrangle but there is some evidence that they may have been at one time linked on the south side by another building which has completely disappeared. Near the houses is an extensive walled garden, and all the indications are that it was a house of considerable importance at one time. The older of the two houses, despite its deteriorating condition shows signs of past grandeur with what would have once been a "grand room" on the first floor, with an ornately plastered and high ceiling. The remains of what were probably the kitchens (the recesses in the walls for the ovens can be seen) are beneath this room which may have been the "banqueting hall". Access to the upper rooms is by an unusual circular wooden staircase enclosed within a square stone tower built outwith but part of the main wall of the house.

Hay family Coat of Arms

The Hay family has been linked with the civic and the ecclesiastical affairs of the area since at least the fourteenth century. In 1334, one Thomas Hay of Urchny founded a Chaplaincy in the Church of Rathven, John de Haia who was the 1st Lord of the Forest of Enzie married a niece of Robert 2nd and at the end of the century King Robert 3rd gave David Hay the Place of Cullen in a Charter which meant that the Hays held the office of Constable and Grieveship of Cullen. There are references in the records to members of the Hay family being ministers of Rathven parish but it is from the beginning of the 18th century that the story leads to the present day.

The Laird of Rannas at the beginning of the century was Charles Hay who was born in 1688. He attended Aberdeen University at the age of fourteen and married Helen Fraser in 1710, producing a son Andrew (born 1713), another son Alexander and six daughters. Charles was an ardent Jacobite but he did not take an active part in the '15 rebellion. He nevertheless surrendered himself to the authorities after the collapse of the rising and after being imprisoned for a short time he was allowed to go peacefully home.

It is on record that in 1733, Andrew took sasine (which is a form of registration of heritable property under Scottish Law) on the estate of Rannas on a crown charter which reserved the life-rents of his father Charles and of his mother. It is also noted that in 1742 he swore allegiance to King George but he took up arms for the Jacobite cause in the '45 rebellion. Physically he was a remarkable man, being about 7 feet tall. He was amongst the first of the Highland army to enter Manchester. As a result the good citizens of the town were very impressed and were convinced that all highlanders were big and to be feared!

After Culloden Andrew Hay was a hunted man but, because the main effort was against the highlanders of Invernesshire and Argyleshire, he was less harried in his own area at first. Soon he had to take to the hills, including the Bin, hiding in the rocks, caves and amongst the heather. Andrew's great size made concealment difficult and there is a story of how he was hunted to a farm kitchen where the lady of the house put two beds end to end and covered him up with bedding.The lady told the searching soldiers that two of her maids were ill with the fever and must not be disturbed, and the soldiers, in fear of the fever did not closely examine the contents of the beds!

Andrew was on the run for five long years, sometimes on the Bin of Cullen and sometimes further afield as far as Kininvie in Banffshire 15 miles away until 1751 when his father died. Perhaps because Andrew's father Charles had not "gone out" in 1715, the government did not confiscate the property nor damage it in any way. Now that Andrew was the laird, and a fugitive, he decided that his best move would be to retire to the continent, leaving his mother to run the estate.

While Andrew was away, in 1759, his home was destroyed by fire and the event is recorded thus in the Scots Magazine - "On 7 May early in the morning the house of Rannas in the Parish of Enzie Banffshire was burned to the ground by accidental fire". Fortunately all the occupants escaped with their lives but nothing was saved except the family papers which were stored in a specially built vault, the location of which is not known. Andrew corresponded with his mother about the rebuilding, saying that if he had been on the spot he would have built on a new site because he did not think there was much saving in using the old stones. Andrew remarked that they would be damaged after two fires but there is no record at all of any previous fire. The damage could not have been too great because the stones were reputedly used to build a new school in Cullen Square about 1820.

In letters to his mother, Andrew said he would have liked to build further from the precipice which is probably the gully to the west of the house where a burn runs down towards the sea. The house was rebuilt in two years, being completed in 1761 and was occupied by Andrew after he made his peace with the authorities and was pardoned. Andrew never married and lived at Rannas with his sister Jean until his death in 1789. Jean continued to live at Rannas until 1790 although the estate had passed into the hands of the Earl of Findlater on 30 April 1781. Andrew apparently had a bond for the price granted by Dr William Thom of Aberdeen for £22,467 sterling. At Whitsuntide 1790 there was a sale of the effects and the house remained empty and neglected. The Earl of Findlater seemingly had scant regard for it and little respect for the care exercised in its rebuilding by Helen Fraser. Jean went to live for a time in Elgin and eventually settled down in Portsoy. She never married.

The link with Leith Hall near Kennethmont originated with Mary, one of Andrew's sisters, who married John Leith of Leith Hall and their son Alexander became heir to his uncle Andrew Hay. Alexander later became a quite famous General but was deeply in debt. Andrew used the money from the sale of Rannas to settle Alexander's financial problems. In return, Andrew's family name Hay was perpetuated by being incorporated in the name Leith-Hay. Andrew, it will be remembered had no family.

Plaque to the Hays of Rannas in Rathven Kirk Yard

There is some uncertainty about what happened to the house built by Helen Fraser while her son Andrew was a fugitive. Undoubtedly it was neglected after it passed into the hands of the Earl of Findlater and, as has been stated earlier it is believed that stones from Rannas were used to build a new school in Cullen. The west building on the site today may well be of 1750-1800 vintage but its mirror-image is of much more recent construction. Almost certainly the wall of the garden is ancient and was probably built at or before Andrew's time. There is every indication that it was once well cared for and played an important part in the running of the estate.

The nearby farm of Rannas is now abandoned and moving towards being ruinous but shows evidence of having, in fairly recent times been a well-developed farm with a water-powered mill attached.

Andrew Hay, the giant of a man who had a very exciting life, travelling as far as Derby with the Jacobite Army, striking terror into the folk of' Manchester, hiding in the Bin of Cullen area as a fugitive before finally fleeing overseas, lies buried under the remains of the aisle in the old kirk at Rathven. All that is left of the old kirk is the aisle in which is a memorial plaque to the Hays of Rannas. The once-famous family of Hay is now no more than a memory but a memory with an interesting story behind it. In the National Trust property of Leith Hall part of a display is dedicated to Andrew Hay and one item on display is one of his huge stockings.

THE TEMPLE OF FAME or POMONA

The Temple was erected in 1822 on a hillock within the Seafield policies, and is visible from the main road to Fochabers. It is a rotunda carried on eight Ionic columns and it originally housed a statue of the goddess Fame. It was restored in 1981 by the Historic Buildings Council for Scotland.

An interesting feature of the building is that under the floor is a room which could be heated. This was used by members of the Seafield family as a room for changing prior to going down a private path, through a tunnel under the main road to the beach.

This practice must have ceased when the railway was built because there is no tunnel under the high embankment.

CHARLIE THE CULLEN HERMIT

This is a compilation by Len Hall of the research work and writings of several members of the Heritage Group, including James G Addison, David Mair, Arnold Pirie and John Rennie. They gleaned their information from newspapers of the time and from people who were involved with Charlie during his time in Cullen.

Up to the time of the second world war and for a number of years afterwards, Cullen had a thriving holiday trade and visitors came from far and wide to enjoy the fresh air, the beach, golf, tennis, not to mention its famous ice cream. One of the attractions in the twenties and early thirties was to enjoy a walk along the cliff path to the east towards Findlater Castle and to pay a visit to the strange little man who lived in a crude hut built on the foreshore against the cliffs. He was known to one and all as Charlie the Hermit and he lived there from November 1920 until he was moved on by the authorities in August 1933, becoming a legend in his own lifetime. This is the story of his life, or as much of it as the members of the Heritage Group can ascertain.

According to an elderly person whose family befriended Charlie after his arrival in Cullen and to whom he confided the story of his life, his name was Marioni and he had been born in Paris of a French mother and an Italian father. During the first world war Charlie Marioni had served in the French navy but he did not like the navy (and the navy did not like him) so he deserted when his ship paid a visit to Plymouth. Surprisingly, since it was wartime he managed to exist undetected while living a nomadic life skulking amongst the rocks and caves of the south coast. If questioned casually about himself it is said he claimed to be Welsh and used the common Welsh name of Moodie.

Scared of being arrested as a deserter of an allied country he kept on the move, crossing to the east coast and moving north as far as Burntisland where he stayed for some time. Moving north again he reached Buckie and then turned round until just east of Cullen, past Portlong and the salmon bothy, round Logie Head and before reaching Sunnyside he found a spot to his liking and decided to stay. It was a lonely place he chose but it had the necessities, a cleft in the rocks at the foot of a high cliff, a well with good water and some fertile land around; at all events this spot was his home for the next 13 years. He developed the cleft in the rocks (it was not really a cave) by putting on a porch and installing "furniture", all made from washed-up material, driftwood and ships' equipment. At that time when fishing was in the doldrums it was quite common for skippers or owners to run unwanted boats on to the shore at lonely spots to save the cost of having them broken up, letting the wind and waves do it for them. Bits and pieces, such as galley equipment found their way into Charlie's shack. He cultivated several bits of ground around his shack and walled them with rocks and stones to grow potatoes and other vegetables for his own use and to sell to local retailers. He caught and dried fish as well as snaring rabbits on the cliff faces to sell to his visitors. It is believed that he had an arrangement with a local chemist who gave him a supply of photographs of himself, standing outside his cave and sales of these along with fish and rabbits provided cash for his needs.

Over the years Charlie and his shack became part of the landscape and locals and visitors alike became accustomed to dropping in for a chat on their way along the coastal path for a walk. He seems to have been a man of amiable disposition and doubtless people gave him little treats like home baking because they felt sorry for him. He was reputed to be a vegetarian with a liking for continental food but it is unlikely that there was much of that in Cullen in those days.

General view of Charlie's "estate"

There is little doubt that he had a steady stream of visitors in the summer months but he must have had a very lonely life during the winter months when all he had around him were the seabirds and the occasional seal and the only sounds he heard were the howling of the wind, the crash of the sea on the rocks, the screaming of the gulls and perhaps the mewing of the two cats who shared his home with him.

It is difficult to visualise how a man could have spent 13 years living under these circumstances. So what sort of a man was this Charlie Marioni? Was he just an unregistered foreigner, a deserter from his country's armed forces who escaped detection by lying low and behaving himself, a man who contributed nothing by way of rates and taxes to the running of his adopted country while at the same time asking nothing from it? Or was he just a man of independent mind who deliberately chose to keep his own company, to be a bother to no-one and who wished to be left alone to eventually die in his isolation?

After more than 60 years, it is not easy to be very definite about the man, his true character and his reasons for adopting such a life-style. Most contemporary reports were written at the time of his arrest, trial, conviction and 'banishment' when there was very definitely a wave of sympathy for Charlie and a degree of anger with the people who had reported him to the authorities. There was a realisation that once his presence was formally reported to the authorities it was inevitable that action had to be taken and there was a recognition that he had been dealt with as lightly and kindly as possible. The scene at Cullen station on the day of his departure reflected the affection which the citizens of Cullen had for him. He was upset at leaving his home of 13 years and having to say goodbye to and then drown his cat, his sole shack companion. But the fact that so many people had come to the station to shake his hand and wish him luck cheered him up. Was he glad that he was moving on to a different life and was he pleased his isolation had ended?

Many questions about Charlie remain unanswered. Although always pleasant to people he was reticent about his past. From what has been gleaned about him, he must have been middle-aged when he deserted from the French navy during the Great War. Why did the authorities ignore the presence of an alien for so long and was it the possibility of war breaking out that brought things to a head? When he appeared before Sheriff More in Banff Sheriff Court on Friday August 25, 1933 to answer a charge of having failed to register as an alien at the time he took up residence on the foreshore at Cullen in 1922, he was smartly dressed in a well-fitting dark suit, with a white shirt and tie, a smart trilby hat and a raincoat over his arm. His whole appearance (he was described in a newspaper report as a dapper little white-bearded old man) belied a life spent in isolation in a remote cave on the edge of the sea. In court it was stated he had £20 in his possession, a considerable sum to have accumulated in those days from his minor sidelines.

He is reputed to have been no mean performer on the fiddle although there is no written evidence of him performing in public, at his cave or elsewhere. One newspaper report said he was a considerable correspondent and received a fortnightly letter from a young Cullen man in Canada as well as others from the United States. The same report described him as a keen reader who read by the light of candles made of his home-made wax which contained his own secret ingredients.

In court it was made clear that Charlie had behaved himself well during his time at Sunnyside but was living in his shelter and cultivating bits of ground without permission. It was also made very clear that the real reason for his being in court was because the large number of people visiting him had disturbed crops and cattle belonging to Mrs Murray who farmed at the head of the cliff. Seafield Estates who owned the land supported her complaint. There was resistance to the idea of putting

Charlie playing his fiddle outside his "home"

an old man into prison and Sheriff More fined him 20 shillings on the understanding that he would go to Banff to register himself as an alien. Charlie said he would go to France and the trial ended with a linguistic exchange, the Sheriff wishing Charlie "Bon voyage" and Charlie replying "Merci bien monsieur". But instead of going to Banff, Charlie went to Leith to see the French Consul about returning to France.

But like everything connected with Charlie there is a strange twist to the tale. An old man of ninety, who was a close friend of Charlie claimed that Charlie never went to France but was sent to an internment camp in the south of England. He is believed to have died there in 1937, his death perhaps hastened by the complete change from his previous free life on the seashore to close confinement. It is said he was buried in a pauper's grave.

The Banffshire Herald of September 21 1933 reported that his shack had been demolished (it is believed by the authorities), the outer walls and roof pulled down and burned. All that remained of what had been Charlie's home for 13 years was a hole in the rock. In 1994 John Rennie, a member of the Cullen Deskford and Portknockie Heritage Group took video pictures of the site for the Group's records. The garden plots can still be identified and the well which was Charlie's water supply is still running and the scorch marks made by the final fire are still visible.

Whatever he was, whoever he was, whether he had a sinister reason for being there will probably never be known but Charlie Marioni (if that was his real name) has a place in the folklore of Cullen in a way that more important people have not. At least he was a character and a tough one at that. What a pity he did not spend some of his time writing down, by the light of his home-made candles during the lonely and wild winter evenings, the real authentic story of Charlie Marioni, the Hermit of Cullen.

CHANGED DAYS - FOR THE BETTER!

Without doubt living conditions are very much better than they were a few years ago. It is within living memory of many people that the town's rubbish was dumped into the sea, from the jetty along Portlong Road, barely a mile from Cullen's famed beach where thousands of holiday makers were enjoying a swim. On the edge of Seatown, admittedly on the lee side of the prevailing wind stood the town's gasworks, wafting into the atmosphere a mixture of obnoxious gases, some with the smell of rotten eggs and others which caught the back of the throat. Nearly every house had at least one coal fire with the result that on damp windless days the atmosphere was thick with smoke. It is quite remarkable the improvement which has taken place.

What will people say about us when they look back at our today, fifty years on? Perhaps by that time we will have ceased to pollute the atmosphere with engine exhaust gases. Our energy source might be drawn from the hot core of the earth or direct from the sun or from the atom. They may think the way we live today is awful!

SOME INTERESTING CULLEN DATES

by Betty Imlah

Betty Imlah is a retired teacher who has a great interest in the history of Cullen. She has made up this list of dates of interesting events which have taken place over the last two centuries.

1811 James, 7th Earl of Findlater and 4th Earl of Seafield died and was succeeded by his cousin Sir Lewis Alexander Grant as 5th Earl of Seafield.

1814 Small Methodist Chapel built with stones carried in creels from the beach.

1819 Cullen harbour established at a cost of £4000.

1820 A start was made by the Earl of Seafield to move the town from Old Cullen to its present site around the Square. The move took ten years to complete.

1820 Toll road was made.

1821 New school in the Square was opened, the building stones coming from Old Rannas House. The school is now a house named "Aldersyde".

1821 The Market Cross was moved from the old town to Castle Hill.

1822 The first steamer seen in the Moray Firth was the "Brilliant".

1822 Temple of Pomona or Fame was built.

1823 The Cullen Hotel (the Seafield Arms) was completed at a cost of £3000. It was built by the Earl of Seafield.

1824 Tochineal Distillery founded by Alexander Wilson.

1825 The slaughterhouse on Skemmels Brae was built.

1828 Tochineal Distillery greatly enlarged.

1829 New cemetery to the east of Cullen opened.

1829 Salmon bothy built at Portlong.

1830 Free Kirk Manse (now Windyridge) built.

1830 Claypots bridge built.

1834 Harbour enlarged.

1837 Sir James Clark of Cullen appointed physician-in-ordinary to Queen Victoria.

1838 Cullen Gas Light Company established.

1840 James, 5th Earl of Seafield died and was succeeded by his brother Francis William Grant-Ogilvie as 6th Earl of Seafield.

1843 Free Church School started in the building used presently (1997) as the Post Office.

1852 Burgh of Cullen appoints its first Police Officer.

1855 Cullen Curling Club formed.

1859 Streets of Cullen lit by gas.

1859 Library and newsroom opened.

1861 Cathay House Built by William Ross who made his fortune as a tea merchant in China.

1865 Main Drain from Rannas to Cullen completed after 6 years work.

1867 North of Scotland Bank built.

1870 Tochineal Distillery moved to Arradoul Buckie.

1871 William Cramond appointed Headmaster of Cullen School (149 pupils).

1872 Market Cross moved to Square.

1874 Seafield Farmhouse built.

1875 Blantyre House built (was The Wakes and now Wakefield Nursing Home).

1875 The telegraph system came to Cullen.

1876 Cullen Public School opened (now the Community Centre).

1880 "The Annals of Cullen" by William Cramond published.

1881 Sir John Charles Ogilvie-Grant, 7th Earl of Seafield died and was succeeded by Ian Charles Ogilvie-Grant as 8th Earl of Seafield.

1884 Building of viaducts completed.

1884 Ian Charles Ogilvie-Grant, 8th Earl of Seafield died.

1885 "Reidhaven" built in Seafield Place as U.P.manse.

1885 Concrete pavements laid in Seafield Street for the first time.

1886 Opening of railway to Cullen.

1888 Two arches of viaducts between Seafield Street and Castle Street collapsed.

1890 Portknockie Harbour opened by Lady Seafield.

1890 Riot at 96 Seatown because of eviction of a publican.

1890 Slaughterhouse moved to Victoria Street (site of present fire station).

1891 "Palm Cottage" in Seafield Place built by sail maker Sandy Ledingham.

1892 Hall-church built in Seafield Place.

1893 Vessel "Glide" of Cullen lost with Skipper Adam Addison and all hands.

1894 Schooner "Jean Shearer" lost behind west pier.

1895 Collection of coins bequeathed to Cullen by John Stuart, Merchant.

1895 Appointment of John Runcie as Harbourmaster.

1896 First golf clubhouse built.

1897 Police Station built in Seafield Street.

1898 Post Office moved to the Square.

1900 Seafield Free Church opened.

1901 Bell for Church donated by Dr George Duffus, in memory of his father Provost William Duffus.

1902 Bowling and Tennis Club opened.

1904 Reidhaven United Presbyterian Church and Seafield Free Church joined to form the Seafield United Free Church.

1904 Dr Cramond resigned as Headmaster of Cullen School for health reasons.

1905 Methodist Church built in Seatown.

1905 Mr Ewan appointed Headmaster of Cullen School.

1905 The telephone came to Cullen.

1909 King Edward V11 visited Cullen.

1910 Town Clock presented to Cullen. (The Lawrence Clock gifted by Dr Lawrence of Chester in memory of his father, a native of Lintmill).

1911 Mr Ewan, Headmaster of Cullen school resigned.

1920 Cullen War Memorial unveiled.

1920 Union Bank moved into new premises in Portknockie.

1921 James Innes appointed Harbourmaster.

1929 Seafield United Free Church joined with Parish Church forming one Cullen Church of Scotland.

1931 Lighthouse erected at harbour.

1931 Foot-bridge erected at Cullen Burn.

1933 Aultmore water scheme to supply Cullen with water was commissioned.

1933 Charlie the Hermit (Charles Marioni) left Cullen after being found guilty of being an unregistered alien.

1934 Townswomen's Guild formed.

1937 Reverend John Guthrie appointed Parish minister.

1937 Charlie the Hermit died in England.

1941 Auxiliary Fire Service established in Cullen.

1942 Cullen Town Hall gutted by fire.

1946 Nina, Countess of Seafield came into her inheritance of Seafield Estates.

1948 Amenities Association founded.

1953 The Great Storm - the Black Shed, Willie Gardiner's boat shed destroyed.

1955 Pageant to celebrate Cullen's quincentenary.

1959 Cylindrical object washed up at new sea wall. This was thought to be a mine. It was removed by a bomb disposal squad from Rosyth.

1960 Caravan site opened.

1961 Queen Elizabeth and Duke of Edinburgh visited Cullen.

1962 Provost Lewis Bain given Freedom of the Burgh.

1967 Cullen Church of Scotland linked with Deskford Church.

1967 Cullen boundary extended to include the Links, the ground having been gifted to the town by the Earl of Seafield.

1968 The railway closed.

1969 Nina, Lady Seafield died and was succeeded by the present Earl (the 13th).

1970 Administration of Burghs of Cullen, Banff, Portsoy, Portknockie and Aberchirder amalgamated.

1970 New Primary School opened. Cullen Higher Grade Public School closed.

1972 Seafield Sportings Club for wealthy sportsmen started - fishing and shooting.

1972 Tourist Office opened.

1972 Cullen designated a Conservation Area.

1972 End of archaeological dig at Green Castle Portknockie.

1975 End of Cullen Town Council - Cullen became part of Moray District.

1975 Earl of Seafield left Cullen House and moved to Old Cullen. Three day auction of the contents of Cullen House.

1975 Freedom of Burgh bestowed on Professor William McHardy and the Earl of Seafield.

1979 Sperm whale weighing about twelve tons stranded on Cullen beach.

1980 Campbell Home closed and converted into flats.

1981 Temple of Pomona restored by Historic Buildings Council for Scotland.

1986 Rev. John Guthrie died. He had been parish minister for 49 years (since 1937).

1986 Spire of former United Free Church restored.

1987 Fire destroyed part of Cullen House.

1987 First Festival of Arts, Crafts and Hobbies.

1989 Two picnic tables installed at harbour, one gifted by Buckie Rotary Club and one by Police Chief Superintendent George Runcie of Cullen.

1989 Cullen House restored after fire.

1989 Tony Hetherington constructed the Giant Steps on cliff path to Findlater Castle at Logie.

1989 New English Bible published. Rev. Professor William McHardy, who was director of the team involved in the publication presented a pulpit copy for use in Cullen Church.

1990 Cullen Deskford and Portknockie Heritage Group founded.

1990 Cullen first had Christmas lights.

1991 Bayview Court Sheltered Housing complex opened.

1992 Dutch Flowerbulb Garden at Deskford opened.

1996 Dutch Flowerbulb Garden closed.

"DEEIN' THE MESSAGES" IN THE 1950'S

by Sandra Taylor

In this short item Sandra recalls the days of her youth in Cullen when she was entrusted with going for the family messages on a Saturday morning. The names of the various shops and shopkeepers will doubtless stir memories of the fifties.

In the fifties, supermarkets were an unimaginable shopping concept. As a youngster, on a Saturday morning I would be bidden "G'wa up the toon for the messages". Armed with the "linie", that vital written instruction as to what to buy, and with the princely sum of 17/6d (87.5p), I planned this expedition with precision so as to take the least possible time out of my precious day.

At that time in Cullen no less than three bakers competed for custom - Reid's, Young's, and McKenzie's. Jim Forbes and Cecil Shearer, purveyors of butcher meat, used well-worn wooden blocks for cutting and chopping and sawdust on the floor - and never heard of E-coli!

Groceries were supplied by Messrs. Ingram, Slater, Forbes and Grant - all on Seafield Street and supplying the popular Syrup of Figs among other medicinal needs were two chemists - James McBeath and E J Balfour.

Anything from a pair of fully-fashioned nylons to 2 yards of table baize to a Sunday costume with matching hat could be purchased from Robertson's or Charlie Gray, Drapers.

All things electrical were supplied and repaired by W G Davidson, while Gair's and Gregor's, at opposite ends of Seafield Street vied with one another to supply hardware requirements.

Folk were shod by the Mustard brothers, Willie, Peter, Dod and John who together with "Andra" Taylor stocked boots and shoes and repaired them.

Bill Christie, barber must have executed countless short-back-and-sides in his time at what is now Cullen Corner Shop, and "ben the hoose" I can distinctly remember Muriel Fraser, ladies' hairdresser, transforming me into a Shirley Temple look-a-like when she gave me my first "Toni".

Curiously, although I always set about the "messages" with due vim and vigour, invariably the task took most of the morning. The queues were long and the banter couthy. There were other diversions - I met chums and blethered - and there was one occasion when, as I trailed doon the Skemmels Brae, I wondered how I was going to explain that "the safties were a' deen" before I made it to Young's.

CULLEN AULD KIRK

Gray's Elegy might have been written here where the centuries-old Kirk stands surrounded by ancient gravestones in a secluded and peaceful corner of the Grounds of the ancestral home of the Earls of Seafield.

Here 'Each in his narrow cell for ever laid
the rude Forefathers of the hamlet sleep.'
and 'All the air a solemn stillness holds'.

Only the song of birds breaks the stillness, but it was not always so in the days before the Royal Burgh of Cullen was moved in 1820-30 to its present site by the sea. In the early part of its chequered history the Kirk was not yet the cruciform building of later times; it was a small rectangular chapel dedicated to the Virgin Mary, and it stood in the centre of the long busy cobbled street that was Cullen then. To the sounds of commerce and play were added the sacred sounds of the Mass, Matins and Vespers when the chapel became a Collegiate Church in 1543; it then had a Provost, 6 Prebendaries and 2 Singing Boys.

Sounds which can only be described as sacrilegious might have been heard in April 1746 when the Duke of Cumberland on his way to Culloden in his pursuit of the Jacobites halted in Old Cullen and stabled his horses in the Kirk. Now since the Reformation of 1560 the Psalms and Hymns of Presbyterian worship are the sounds heard each Sunday in our beautiful Auld Kirk.

THE OLD CHURCH OF DESKFORD

In a quiet corner of the churchyard in Kirktown of Deskford can be seen the remains of an ancient church dedicated to St John. There was a chapel in Deskford at the time of Robert the Bruce but the oldest part of this church may date from 1437. It contains an 8 ft. high sacrament house, of the finest freestone and bearing the date 1551. Both survived the Reformation of 1560 and the church and sacrament house are protected as ancient monuments. It was unroofed when the present Deskford Church was built in 1872. Next door can be seen the remains of what was once the proud Deskford Castle.

THE REVEREND JOHN T. GUTHRIE

On the wall facing the pulpit in the Auld Kirk of Cullen there is a plaque which reads: "To the Glory of God and Sacred to the Memory of the Reverend John T. Guthrie M.A., J.P., 1908 - 1985, for almost half a century the faithful and well-loved Minister of this Church". It might have read "with affection and admiration", for it represented the final gesture of his numerous friends in the Parishes of Cullen and Deskford, indeed of many outwith the place he served so long.

Born at Findhorn, the son of the Manse, Mr Guthrie was classical Dux at Robert Gordon's in Aberdeen. After graduating M.A. at the University of Aberdeen, he was a student of Law for a short time, but eventually he went to Glasgow University to study Theology. His first appointment was as Assistant Minister at Paisley High Church, and it was from there he came to preach for Cullen Old. That was the start of a long and very effective ministry. As a pastor and preacher he was held in high regard

For many years he was a trusted Presbytery and Synod Clerk. He was chaplain of the local school, a member of the Town Council, a stalwart on the golf course and on the bowling green.

An old lady summed up the friendly feelings he evoked when she said "The manse door was aye open".

CULLEN BURGH CROSS

The Burgh Cross which stands in the Square in Cullen dates from 1696 although the carving of the Virgin and Child on the front is reputedly older. It is recorded that it stood outside the Auld Kirk gates when it was the centre of the old town of Cullen. The town then comprised one long street which followed roughly the line of the present drive from Grant Street leading to Cullen House and continued eastwards towards the Toll House at the top end of Cullen.

It seems it had taken twenty years to construct the Cross, for two masons received an initial payment from the town Baillies in 1675 and twenty years later, in 1695 a Cullen mason Lauchlan McPetter made a contract with the Baillies "anent the building, finishing and fitting the cross".

It remained outside the church until the 1820s when the Earl of Seafield decided to erect a new town on the present site of Cullen. The old town was in a ruinous state and was demolished.

Around this time the Cross was dismantled and re-erected on the Castle Hill, overlooking the Seatown of Cullen where it stood until 1872 when it was again dismantled and placed in its present site in the Square.

On the back cover of this book is a photograph of the Burgh Cross.